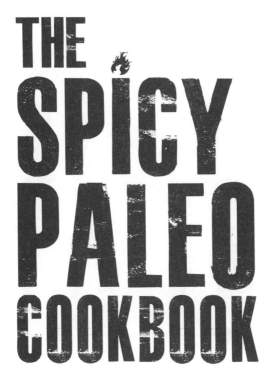

THE SPICY PALEO COOKBOOK

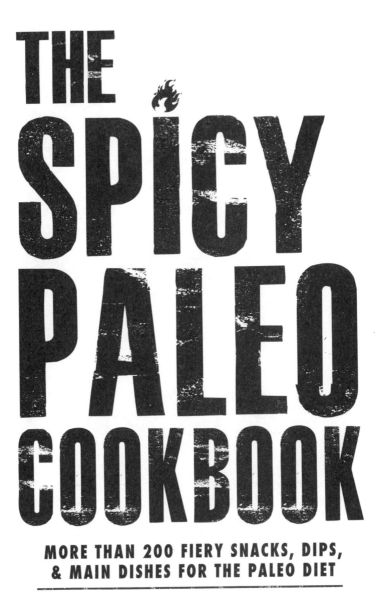

THE SPICY PALEO COOKBOOK

MORE THAN 200 FIERY SNACKS, DIPS, & MAIN DISHES FOR THE PALEO DIET

Emily Dionne, MS, RD, LDN, CSSD, ACSM-HFS, and **Erin Ray**

Adamsmedia
Avon, Massachusetts

Dedication

For the eternal Ten Spot

Published by
Adams Media, a division of F+W Media, Inc.
57 Littlefield Street, Avon, MA 02322 U.S.A.
www.adamsmedia.com

Contains material adapted and abridged from *The Everything® Paleolithic Diet Slow Cooker Cookbook* by Emily Dionne, copyright © 2013 by F+W Media, Inc., ISBN 10: 1-4405-5536-2, ISBN 13: 978-1-4405-5536-7.

ISBN 10: 1-4405-7433-2
ISBN 13: 978-1-4405-7433-7
eISBN 10: 1-4405-7434-0
eISBN 13: 978-1-4405-7434-4

Printed in the United States of America.

10   9   8   7   6   5   4   3   2   1

Library of Congress Cataloging-in-Publication Data

Dionne, Emily.
  The spicy Paleo cookbook / Emily Dionne, MS, RD, LDN, CSSD, ACSM-HFS, and Erin Ray.
      pages cm
  ISBN 978-1-4405-7433-7 (pb) -- ISBN 1-4405-7433-2 (pb) -- ISBN 978-1-4405-7434-4 (ebook) -- ISBN 1-4405-7434-0 (ebook)
  1. High-protein diet--Recipes. 2. Prehistoric peoples--Nutrition. 3. Cooking (Hot pepper sauces) 4. Cooking (Spices) I. Ray, Erin. II. Title.
  RM237.65.D56 2014
  641.6'383--dc23

                    2014000096

This book is available at quantity discounts for bulk purchases.
For information, please call 1-800-289-0963.

Acknowledgments

First and foremost, we would like to thank our family, friends, and colleagues for believing in us and pushing us to always be the best version of ourselves; specifically the Dionne Family, the Toole and McFadden Family, the Ray Family, and the Brown Family. Thank you for your patience during this process and for unknowingly serving as guinea pigs for our extra-spicy recipe experiments!

A special thank you to C.J. Ray, for being an amazingly loving husband and quite brutally honest taste tester! Your uncanny ability to contribute some of your creativity helped make those many late-night working sessions more than just tolerable. Your support and encouragement made this project a huge success. To Buddy, as always, your patience and unconditional love is immeasurable.

Finally, a special thank you to Adams Media for this opportunity. We are so proud to have embarked on this wonderful and delicious journey!

CONTENTS

Chapter 3: Soups, Stews, and Chilis 75

Chapter 4: Entrées 95

Chapter 5: Sides... 143

Chapter 6: Snacks.. 171

Chapter 7: Desserts and Drinks 199

INTRODUCTION

Tired of eating the same old thing every day? Sick of bland, tasteless food? Want to spice up your cooking? Today, spicy ingredients are putting a fire underneath the seats of the finest gourmet chefs and diner line cooks alike! However, finding Paleo dishes that ignite that flame in your own kitchen can be hard to find. Fortunately, *The Spicy Paleo Cookbook* gives you more than 200 recipes that will bring the heat right to the comfort of your own home!

These spicy recipes, such as Red Hot Ratatouille, Wasabi-Crusted Tuna, and Cardamom Carrot Custard, can really add spice to your life! Whether you're looking for main courses packed full of zing; sides, salads, and soups that are sure to knock your socks off; or decadent desserts that create the perfect balance between sugar and spice, you've come to the right place. The range of recipes throughout—like the Spicy Carrot Fries, Pepper-Crusted Steak, and Fiery Fried Figs— are much more than just spicy. The fresh herbs, spices, seasonings, hot peppers, and other unique, mouthwatering ingredients generate a wide-ranging variety of exceptional flavors, distinct aromas, and diverse cuisines—all of which add up to varying degrees of *hot*!

You'll find the spectrum of spices—ranging from fierce, hot, and fiery to tart, honeyed, and gingerly spiced—all add a deliciously unique dimension to some otherwise basic Paleolithic fare. Some of the recipes, like the Pumpkin Spice Pancakes, will tickle your taste buds with just a hint of cinnamon and pumpkin pie spice, while the heat from others, like the Chipotle Tomato Sauce, is sure to make your eyes water! Whether you're looking for something mild, medium, or just plain *hot*, the choice is yours. From breakfast, lunch, and dinner cuisine, to late night zesty treats, with the irresistible recipes of *The Spicy Paleo Cookbook*, your palate will never be same!

CHAPTER 1

Breakfast and Brunch

Breakfast is commonly referred to as the most important meal of the day, but if you're like many people, you might not have the time or motivation to prepare it each day. However, with the spicy, eye-opening, and flavorful dishes found in this chapter, you'll finally be excited to get out of bed! Here you'll find hot and spicy, well-balanced breakfast and brunch dishes like the Fiery Frittata, Sizzling Chorizo and Egg Casserole, and the Southwestern Omelet that will refuel your body and brain and improve your cognitive ability and energy. The recipes for Paleo muffins, baked egg dishes, smoothies, and more range from savory and mild to super-spicy. These breakfast creations will more than satisfy your Paleolithic palate. The combination of different herbs and spices in each dish add layers of deep flavor and really heat up those boring, everyday breakfast and brunch dishes. So start your morning right with these hot and spicy Paleo dishes!

Fiery Fruit Salad

This Fiery Fruit Salad may be a nontraditional way of eating fruit, but it's sure to tantalize your senses with the cool sweetness of fruit combined with heat from the Sriracha. If that combination isn't enough for your taste buds, the cilantro and mint reinforce this sweet and spicy tandem perfectly! Try this recipe with other fruits, like mango slices, strawberries, cantaloupe, or whatever pleasures your palate.

Serves 8–10

2 apples, halved and thinly sliced

2 pears, halved and thinly sliced

½ pineapple, peeled, cored, and thinly sliced

3 kiwis, peeled and thinly sliced

¼ cup fresh lime juice

¼ cup fresh orange juice

½ teaspoon Sriracha sauce

2 tablespoons freshly chopped cilantro

2 tablespoons freshly chopped mint

1 teaspoon orange zest

½ teaspoon raw organic honey

1 tablespoon white wine vinegar

1. Place sliced fruit on serving platter, slightly stacking and alternating with each fruit.

2. In a mixing bowl, combine lime juice, orange juice, Sriracha sauce, cilantro, mint, orange zest, honey, and white wine vinegar. Whisk together until well blended and frothy, and set the vinaigrette aside.

3. Pour spicy vinaigrette over fruit and serve immediately.

Cinnamon Spice Paleo Muffins

These super-tasty Cinnamon Spice Paleo Muffins are so simple; they're great for breakfast on the go and are equally as satisfying any time of day. The spice from the cinnamon and nutmeg is just right, and it really brings out the sweetness of the more traditional ingredients like honey and applesauce. Store these muffins in an airtight container for up to a week.

1. Preheat the oven to 400°F and grease a standard, 12-cup muffin pan with coconut oil.

2. Add eggs, applesauce, coconut flour, cinnamon, nutmeg, baking soda, and vanilla extract into a medium mixing bowl. Mix with an immersion blender or whisk until well mixed. Let the batter sit to thicken about 3 minutes. Once thick, use ⅓ cup measuring scoop to spoon batter into the muffin pan.

3. Bake 12–15 minutes until muffins start to brown and are not soft when lightly touched on top. Remove from oven and let cool for 2 minutes, then drizzle with honey, if desired.

Yields 6 muffins

Coconut oil (for greasing the pan)
5 large eggs
1 cup homemade applesauce
½ cup coconut flour
2 tablespoons cinnamon
1 teaspoon nutmeg
1 teaspoon baking soda
1 teaspoon vanilla extract
Raw organic honey, for garnish (optional)

🔥 SWEETER BY THE DOZEN!

Do you prefer your muffins a bit sweeter, to help balance out the spice? Go ahead and reduce the applesauce by ¼ cup and add an overripe banana before blending. You can also try adding ½ cup blueberries or strawberries, or even a finely chopped apple to add a little crunch for additional texture.

Zesty Breakfast Sausages

These Paleo sausage patties are so easy to make at home that you'll never buy them at the grocery store again! They pack a huge amount of flavor in just one bite without leaving you feeling guilty from any unwanted additives. The key ingredient in this recipe is the ground fennel. Its licorice-like taste is fresh and bright and beautifully accents the pork. The combination of hot and spicy peppers really completes the zing!

Serves 4

1 pound ground pork
1 teaspoon minced garlic
1 teaspoon ground fennel
1 teaspoon paprika
½ teaspoon black pepper
½ teaspoon sea salt
¼ teaspoon cayenne pepper
2 tablespoons olive oil

1. Combine pork, garlic, and all dry ingredients in a mixing bowl. Make sure all spices are incorporated throughout the pork.

2. Shape pork mixture into small, circular patties (approximately 8 patties).

3. Heat a large skillet to medium heat and add olive oil. Once heated, add the patties to the skillet and cook for approximately 3–4 minutes per side until golden brown. (The middle of the patties should no longer be pink.) Remove from heat and enjoy!

🔥 SPICY SAUSAGE VARIATIONS!

These sausages can be made with any kind of meat and flavor. The choices are endless! Try using turkey, chicken, beef, venison, or bison meat for a different flavor. Jazz up the taste and texture with sautéed onions and garlic, or add spice with allspice or Cajun seasoning. Any flavor combination will go great with eggs and will make a tasty breakfast!

Southwestern Omelet

This flavorful, south-of-the-border-inspired creation is packed with sautéed fresh vegetables and savory sausage patties. This spicy dish will start your day off with a punch of flavor and provide your body with long-lasting energy! The avocado and salsa topping add a cool and creamy texture to balance the heat from the fiery jalapeños and chili powder.

1. Heat 1 tablespoon olive oil over medium heat in a medium nonstick skillet. Add chopped onion, bell pepper, and jalapeño, and cook over medium heat for 5 minutes until softened.

2. Meanwhile, whisk eggs with sea salt, white pepper, and garlic powder in a mixing bowl.

3. Remove vegetables from skillet and set aside.

4. Add ½ tablespoon olive oil to the same skillet and pour in half of the egg mixture. When your omelet is heating, it may bubble. (Remove from heat briefly when this happens to avoid holes in your omelet.) Once your omelet starts to cook through (about 2–3 minutes), add half of the partially cooked veggies, half of the Zesty Breakfast Sausages, and half of the chopped tomato to one side of the omelet.

5. After 1 minute, and once your eggs are solid, flip the egg-only half of your omelet over onto the vegetable-filled half. Cook for 1 minute, and flip the omelet over to cook the other side for 1–2 minutes.

6. Remove from skillet and repeat steps 4–5 for the second half of your egg mixture.

7. Once both omelets are done, top with avocado slices, a dollop of salsa, and a pinch of chopped cilantro.

Serves 2

2–3 tablespoons olive oil
1 medium Spanish onion, chopped
1 red bell pepper, chopped
1 jalapeño, chopped and seeds removed
4–5 large eggs
1 teaspoon sea salt
1 teaspoon white pepper
1 teaspoon garlic powder
4 Zesty Breakfast Sausages, chopped into small bites (see recipe in this chapter)
1 tomato, chopped
1 ripe avocado, peeled, pitted, and sliced
Salsa, to taste
Sprinkle of chopped cilantro, for garnish

Spicy Sweet Potato Home Fries

The smell of these Paleo home fries in the morning is enough to wake even the deepest of sleepers! The smoked paprika and red pepper flakes combined with sweet onion result in the perfect marriage of sweet and spicy. Enjoy the festivities!

Serves 4

1½ tablespoons olive oil
1 medium sweet onion, chopped
3 large sweet potatoes, chopped
  into bite-size chunks
½ teaspoon sea salt
½ teaspoon pepper
½ teaspoon smoked paprika
1 tablespoon minced garlic
1 teaspoon dried red pepper
  flakes

1. Heat a large skillet over medium heat. Once hot, add the oil and chopped onion. (Note: If you don't want the onions crispy and brown, add them once the potatoes have cooked halfway.)

2. Season the sweet potato with salt, pepper, and paprika, then add the sweet potato to the skillet and brown before flipping. Continue to do this until potatoes reach a golden brown hue and you are able to easily pierce them with a fork, about 15 minutes, stirring occasionally.

3. Just before removing from heat, add the minced garlic and red pepper flakes.

🔥 BREAKFAST FOR DINNER

Preheat the oven to 450°F. Instead of cutting the sweet potatoes into small, home fry–size bites, cut them into long strips, to resemble the shape of French fries. Add the potato strips (in a single layer) and the rest of the ingredients in this recipe to a baking dish that has been lightly sprayed with nonstick spray. Bake for 30–40 minutes, or until browned.

Tasty Taco Scramble

This spicy breakfast dish is incredibly easy to make, especially when you have leftover taco meat from dinner the night before! It can also double as a quick and practically effortless super supper. The array of red hot herbs and spices like chili powder, cumin, and cayenne pepper create a sizzling home-made taco seasoning. You'll be asked to make it for years to come!

1. Add lean ground beef to a large skillet over medium heat. Break up the beef in the pan as it browns. Drain excess fat from beef once cooked halfway through, about 2–3 minutes, then add spices to beef and cook until beef is browned. Once browned, remove beef from skillet and place in a separate bowl.

2. In the same skillet over medium heat, add olive oil. Once the oil has heated, add chopped onion and pepper and sauté for 5–7 minutes until the onions are translucent.

3. Meanwhile, add eggs, salt, and water to a mixing bowl and whisk until well blended. Add eggs to skillet and scramble with the vegetables.

4. Remove from heat and serve scrambled eggs over the taco meat. Top with salsa and/or avocado slices for added flavor!

Serves 3–4

½ pound lean ground beef
1 teaspoon paprika
1 teaspoon cumin
1 teaspoon chili powder
1 teaspoon garlic powder
1 teaspoon pepper
¼ teaspoon cayenne pepper
  (add more if you like it hot!)
1 tablespoon olive oil
1 small onion, chopped
1 bell pepper, chopped
3–4 large eggs
½ teaspoon salt
1 tablespoon water
1 cup fresh salsa (optional)
6–8 avocado slices (optional)

Fiery Frittata

Frittatas are the "everything but the kitchen sink" of breakfast foods, and the cumin, chili powder, and serrano pepper used in this Fiery Frittata are so hot, they'll make you want to turn the water on! To mix up this fiery dish, experiment with other proteins, vegetables, and spices to make this the perfect meal for you.

Serves 4

2 tablespoons olive oil
½ medium onion, chopped
1 cup chopped white mushrooms
½ serrano pepper, chopped
1 cup baby spinach
¼ teaspoon garam masala
¼ teaspoon chili powder
¼ teaspoon cumin
4–5 large eggs
Sea salt and pepper, to taste

1. Heat olive oil in a medium skillet over medium heat.

2. Add chopped onion and sauté for 3–4 minutes or until translucent.

3. Add mushrooms and chopped serrano pepper and sauté for about 5 minutes.

4. Add spinach, garam masala, chili powder, and cumin, and stir so the mixture is well blended. The spinach will wilt fast, so keep an eye on it.

5. While the vegetables are cooking, whisk the eggs in a mixing bowl with sea salt and pepper. Pour the eggs into the skillet, turn the heat to medium-low, cover, and cook for 5–7 minutes, or until the eggs are firm.

6. Slide the entire frittata onto a serving platter, slice, and serve!

🔥 THE SLENDER SERRANO

Its size and shape make the serrano pepper difficult to core and seed (where most of the spice is!), so the best way to temper it is by using less of it. Serrano peppers are more than five times hotter than jalapeños, so you can always add more if you like the heat. The small, thin serrano pods can be purchased fresh or canned in supermarkets and ethnic food stores. They are also available in dried form, known as chile seco.

Pumpkin Spice Pancakes

You may think to eat pumpkin in the fall, but these Paleo Pumpkin Spice Pancakes are perfect any time of year! This version is so simple; the cinnamon-spice blend is the perfect combination to completely satisfy your sweet tooth, and you'll want to forever preserve the amazingly delightful aroma that they produce. These pancakes will have you longing for morning, and are absolutely guaranteed to spice up your day!

Serves 2

- ½ cup almond flour
- ¼ cup coconut flour
- ¼ teaspoon baking soda
- ½ tablespoon cinnamon
- 1 teaspoon pumpkin pie spice
- Pinch salt
- ½ cup pumpkin purée
- 3 eggs
- 2 tablespoons raw organic honey
- 1 teaspoon vanilla extract
- Coconut oil (for the griddle/ skillet)
- ¼ cup pure maple syrup

1. Heat a griddle or large skillet over medium heat.

2. Combine all dry ingredients in one mixing bowl, and all wet ingredients except the coconut oil and maple syrup in another bowl. Whisk wet ingredients together, and add to dry ingredients. Stir until well blended.

3. Add coconut oil to the griddle and allow it to melt.

4. Use ⅓ cup measuring scoop (or an ice cream scooper) to spoon pancake mixture onto the griddle. The batter will thicken, so you may not have perfectly round pancakes. Cook for 3–4 minutes on one side, carefully flip, and cook for another 2–3 minutes more. Add more coconut oil to each batch until the batter is gone, then enjoy with a small drizzle of pure maple syrup.

🔥 THE PERFECT PUMPKIN PASTRY

If you want to dress up these Paleo delights, just roll up the warm pancakes, top with a dollop of cold Paleo-approved coconut milk whipped cream, and finish with a drizzle of maple syrup, raspberry sauce, or warm hazelnut sauce, and fresh berries or roasted almonds!

Buffalo Chicken Breakfast Muffins

These hot little protein muffins are a perfect way to spice up your morning! They are super easy to make and are a great hot or cold "grab and go" option for workdays. Use cupcake/muffin liners (silicon also works great!) when baking these hot and spicy Buffalo Chicken Breakfast Muffins to prevent the egg from sticking to your muffin tin. If you want to make these fiery muffins even hotter, feel free to vary the amount of hot sauce based on the level of heat you desire.

Yields 6 muffins

Pinch salt and pepper
2 chicken breasts
3 tablespoons clarified butter, melted
¼ cup hot sauce (Frank's Red Hot works well)
6 large eggs
¼ teaspoon garlic powder

1. Preheat the oven to 425°F.

2. Sprinkle salt and pepper on chicken breasts, then place on a baking sheet sprayed with nonstick spray. Bake for 20 minutes, or until cooked through.

3. Remove from oven, lower the oven temperature to 350°F, and let the chicken cool for a few minutes, then shred chicken breasts (with two forks) into a small mixing bowl. Add melted clarified butter and hot sauce to shredded chicken.

4. Line a 6-cup muffin tin with muffin liners.

5. In a medium mixing bowl, whisk the eggs and garlic powder, then evenly distribute the egg mixture into the muffin tin. Add the shredded chicken to each muffin. (Do not overflow.) *Note: You may have extra shredded chicken. Feel free to save and use on a salad.*

6. Bake at 350°F for about 30 minutes, or until the eggs start to rise and turn a golden brown.

Cinnamon Pumpkin Spice Breakfast Bars

Enjoy the invigorating flavors of fall with these zesty Cinnamon Pumpkin Spice Breakfast Bars. The balance of sweet pumpkin and spicy cinnamon creates an irresistibly crunchy breakfast, guaranteed to tantalize the palate! The pumpkin pie spice adds a hint of heat, but if you prefer a bit more, just throw in some allspice or a pinch of ground cloves for added zing. These bars are perfect for an on-the-go quick bite, and taste delicious alongside a dark, rich cup of coffee.

Yields 14–16 bars

⅔ cup raw organic honey
3 tablespoons coconut oil
1 teaspoon vanilla extract
Pinch sea salt
½ cup canned pumpkin purée
½ teaspoon cardamom
½ teaspoon cinnamon
½ teaspoon nutmeg
1 cup raw pumpkin seeds (packaged)
1 cup almonds, roughly chopped
1 cup sunflower seeds
1 cup unsweetened shredded coconut

1. Preheat the oven to 300°F.

2. Line a 9" × 13" baking dish with parchment paper.

3. Place a small pot over medium heat, and combine the honey, coconut oil, vanilla extract, and sea salt. Whisk ingredients until blended. Remove pot from heat and whisk in the pumpkin, cardamom, cinnamon, and nutmeg, and set aside.

4. Combine pumpkin seeds, chopped almonds, sunflower seeds, and shredded coconut in a large mixing bowl. Pour the pumpkin/honey mixture over the dry ingredients and stir until nuts and seeds are well coated.

5. Pour mixture into lined baking dish and lightly pat down ingredients with your hand to evenly distribute.

6. Bake for 25–30 minutes, then remove from heat. Cool, then place lined baking dish into the refrigerator for at least 1 hour to set the mixture.

7. Remove from the refrigerator and peel parchment paper off the bottom of the formed mixture. Cut into even slices (cut 4" × 4" slices for 16 bars).

Sizzling Chorizo and Egg Casserole

Chorizo is a zesty Spanish pork sausage with tons of flavor. Its bright red color is due to large amounts of paprika. This delicious breakfast dish really captures the essence of spicy chorizo by incorporating onion, red pepper, and jalapeños. You'll be asked to make this sizzling sensation over and over again!

Serves 12

1 pound spicy ground chorizo
1 tablespoon olive oil
1 medium onion, chopped
1 red bell pepper, chopped
2 small jalapeños, seeded and chopped
10 large eggs
½ teaspoon salt
½ teaspoon pepper
½ teaspoon garlic salt
1 tablespoon dried dill
1 teaspoon clarified butter, softened
1 tablespoon fresh parsley, chopped

1. Preheat the oven to 350°F.

2. Cook chorizo in a large skillet over medium heat, breaking into chunks until browned, about 10 minutes. Transfer cooked chorizo to a bowl and add olive oil to the same skillet. Turn heat up to medium-high.

3. Sauté the onion, bell pepper, and jalapeños for 8 minutes, or until they start to brown.

4. In a large mixing bowl, combine eggs, salt, pepper, garlic salt, and dill. Whisk together until all yolks are broken.

5. Use softened clarified butter to grease 9" × 13" baking dish.

6. Add chorizo to egg mixture and stir, then pour into the baking dish. Bake for 30–40 minutes, or until eggs are set and the top starts to turn golden brown. Garnish with fresh parsley, and slice into 12 pieces.

Spicy Breakfast "Menemen"

This breakfast is inspired by the traditional Turkish dish menemen, which is typically cooked with just eggs, vegetables, and spices. However, the addition of a meat of your choice, like the Paleo-friendly, nitrate-free bacon used here, makes this dish super-satisfying and packed with protein! This combination of peppers, cumin, red pepper flakes, and Tabasco sauce is guaranteed to heat up your morning.

1. In a medium skillet, heat olive oil over medium heat.

2. Add onion, green bell pepper, garlic, diced tomatoes, cumin, salt, pepper, and red pepper flakes. Stir often; sauté for about 10 minutes or until onions are translucent and juice starts to thicken.

3. While vegetables are sautéing, whisk eggs in a bowl and add bacon bits. Add egg mixture to the skillet vegetables and scramble until fully cooked. Top with green onion and Tabasco for a little extra heat. Scoop onto a plate and serve.

Serves 2

2 tablespoons olive oil
½ yellow onion, diced
1 green bell pepper, diced
1 clove garlic, minced
1 (14-ounce) can diced tomatoes (drain ½ of the juice)
½ teaspoon cumin
½ teaspoon salt
½ teaspoon black pepper
¼ teaspoon red pepper flakes
4 eggs, scrambled
4 slices nitrate-free bacon, cooked and crumbled
1 green onion, finely sliced
Tabasco sauce, to taste

Succulent Sweet Potato Hash

This sweet potato dish is the perfect side to any breakfast entrée. This Paleo recipe is loaded with fiery flavor from the delicious combination of onions, peppers, prosciutto, rosemary, and cayenne pepper. The hot and spicy ingredients work seamlessly with the sweet potatoes, creating a glorious harmony of sugar and spice. Enjoy!

Serves 2

2 tablespoons olive oil
½ medium yellow onion, finely diced
1 jalapeño, seeded and finely diced
1 large sweet potato, peeled and shredded
2 pieces prosciutto, browned and chopped into small pieces
½ teaspoon dried rosemary
¼ teaspoon cayenne pepper
Salt and pepper, to taste

1. In a medium skillet, heat olive oil over medium heat. Once hot, add onion and jalapeño and sauté for about 5 minutes.

2. Add shredded sweet potato, prosciutto bits, rosemary, and cayenne pepper to skillet and turn up to medium-high heat. Cook for 20–30 minutes, tossing often and pressing the mixture down into the pan with a spatula to help brown. Once well done and golden brown, season with salt and pepper and serve.

🔥 POACHED EGGS ON HASH

Try using the back of a spoon to create two or three holes in the hash while it is still in the skillet, and then drop an egg into each. Let the eggs fry until they are cooked through and serve immediately. Try this dish alongside the Fiery Fruit Salad (see recipe in this chapter).

Racy Raspberry Paleo Toaster Pastries

These tasty little tarts are perfect for an early morning sweet tooth. The juice and zest from the freshly squeezed orange and lemon give this breakfast pastry a "pop" of tart! Ginger brings the zing to this hot and spicy recipe, along with its numerous health benefits like its anti-inflammatory properties and its helpful role in alleviating and preventing nausea. These can be made ahead, and store well for up to 1 week in the refrigerator.

1. Preheat the oven to 350°F.

2. **For Dough:** Combine the water, clarified butter, maple syrup, vanilla, and sea salt in a small sauce pot and bring to a boil. Remove from heat. Once cooled slightly, place in a mixing bowl and add in almond flour, baking soda, and the mashed banana. Mix until well blended and dough-like.

3. **For Filling:** Add all filling ingredients to a small sauce pot and heat on medium-low heat for about 45 minutes. This will help the flavors meld together and also thicken the filling. Let cool slightly and use an immersion blender to blend into a jam-like consistency.

4. **To Complete:** Roll out the "dough" between parchment or wax paper until smooth and thin (about ¼" thick). Cut into 12 rectangles. Place 6 rectangles on a parchment paper–lined baking sheet. Spoon about 2 tablespoons of the filling onto all 6 pieces of dough. Top these with the remaining 6 rectangles as though you are making a mini sandwich. Bake for 20–25 minutes until slightly browned, checking to make sure they do not burn. Remove from heat and enjoy!

Yields 6 pastries

For Dough:
¼ cup water
¼ cup clarified butter
¼ cup pure maple syrup
1 teaspoon vanilla
Pinch sea salt
1 cup almond flour
¼ teaspoon baking soda
1 extra ripe banana, mashed

For Filling:
2 cups raspberries
½ cup coconut water
Juice of ½ orange
Juice of 1 lemon
1 teaspoon lemon zest
1 teaspoon orange zest
1 tablespoon vanilla extract
1 teaspoon ground ginger

Gingery Walnut Muffins

The ginger and allspice in this recipe give the muffins their added "spice." The cloves get the MVP award, as they are known for providing their uniquely warm, sweet, and aromatic taste to ginger muffins and breads, and they really bring their A-game here! This fall favorite tastes best warmed, served with a mug of spiced tea, like the Masala-Spiced Chai Tea in Chapter 7.

Yields 12 muffins

2 cups coconut flour
½ cup shredded coconut
⅔ cup chopped walnuts
1 teaspoon ground ginger
¼ teaspoon allspice
Pinch ground cloves
5 eggs
¼ cup coconut oil (melted)
¼ cup applesauce
¼ cup raw organic honey
1 tablespoon vanilla extract

1. Preheat the oven to 350°F. In a large mixing bowl, combine all dry ingredients. In a medium mixing bowl, whisk all wet ingredients together until well blended. Add wet ingredients to dry ingredients. Let stand for 3–5 minutes.

2. Line a muffin tin with paper muffin liners and spoon batter into liners. (To make them evenly portioned, use a ½ cup measuring scoop to spoon mixture into muffin tin.)

3. Bake the muffins for 25–30 minutes or until they start to brown on top. Remove from heat and cool. Enjoy!

♠ THE HEALTH BENEFITS OF GINGER

Ginger is often used to treat various types of stomach problems including motion sickness, morning sickness, gas, nausea caused by cancer treatment, and more. In addition, ginger can help relieve arthritis pain and lower back pain, and at times, the fresh juice is applied to the skin to treat burns. Research has even shown that ginger can help relieve menstrual pain in some women.

Zesty Breakfast Smoothie

This nutrient-filled breakfast smoothie is sure to help start your day off right! The ingredients in this smoothie are loaded with antioxidants and vitamins, keeping you satisfied while boosting your immune system. And as if that wasn't amazing enough, the cinnamon and ginger combined with the jalapeños give this smoothie some serious zest! Try adding additional hot peppers or a pinch of cayenne to spice it up another level.

1. Add all ingredients (except for the ice) to a high-powered blender and blend until smooth and foamy.

2. Serve on ice, if desired, in a large glass.

Serves 1

1 banana, chopped (preferably frozen)

1 cup fresh spinach

½ jalapeño, seeded

½ apple (Fuji is great due to its crisp sweetness)

½ cup unsweetened coconut milk

1 cup coconut water

1 tablespoon almond butter

¼ teaspoon cinnamon

Pinch ground ginger

Ice (optional)

Carrot Ginger Smoothie

Smoothies are a great "on-the-go" choice for breakfast. They are easy to prepare, and are even easier to clean up! The ginger and nutmeg make this smoothie a zesty treat that is sure to warm your soul and satisfy your stomach on your morning commute.

Serves 1

1 large carrot, peeled and
  chopped
1 apple, peeled and chopped
½" chunk ginger, grated
Juice of 1 orange
1 teaspoon raw organic honey
¼ teaspoon cinnamon
⅛ teaspoon nutmeg
½ cup water
¼ cup ice

1. Add all ingredients to blender and blend until smooth and foamy.

2. Pour into a large glass and serve immediately.

Spiced Pumpkin Banana Smoothie

This perfect autumnally flavored smoothie is rich and sweet with a bit of zing from the pumpkin pie spice and cardamom. This smoothie will fill you up any time of day and is a sure way to satisfy a sweet craving. The natural sugar from the coconut ingredients and the maple syrup are a perfect match for the cinnamon and spice, making it all taste so nice!

1. Add all ingredients (except for the ice) to a blender and blend until smooth and foamy.

2. Serve on ice in a large smoothie glass.

🔥 A SPOONFUL OF PROTEIN!

Add some vanilla protein powder to make this smoothie the perfect post-workout snack. The protein powder gives an added sweet flavor, and is typically loaded with vitamins and minerals, making this smoothie a guaranteed way to re-charge and re-fuel! Prefer more fiber? Add 1–2 tablespoons of ground flaxseed—this will boost your daily fiber intake, as well as provide a heart-healthy dose of omega-3 fatty acids.

Serves 2

1 banana, peeled (and preferably frozen)
¾ cup pumpkin purée
5 cups unsweetened coconut milk
¾ cup plain unsweetened coconut yogurt
1 tablespoon pure maple syrup
½ teaspoon pumpkin pie spice
½ teaspoon cinnamon
1 teaspoon vanilla extract
½ teaspoon ground cardamom
Ice, to taste

CHAPTER 2

Salads and Hors D'oeuvres

The tempting deep-fried, cheese-stuffed options typically found at family parties and other functions can challenge your adherence to the Paleolithic lifestyle. But with the easy-to-make, hot and spicy appetizer and salad recipes found in this chapter, you won't feel like you're missing out! Whether you're eating Spicy Tuna Salad, Paleo Wild Wings, or Zesty Carrot Dip, you'll know that you're eating delicious, guilt-free, Paleo-approved food that will knock your socks off! In addition to being delicious, each recipe is flexible when it comes to the amount of spice, so take the time to experiment with different types of hot peppers, spices, and herbs to add a little kick to common Paleo-friendly salads and appetizers. Substitute avocados and cauliflower for non-Paleo ingredients like cream and cheese. Add a little sweetness with honey and fruit. Save those extra calories for a glass of wine or a beer, while relishing these spiced-up finger foods!

Peppered Ahi Tuna with Greens

You won't feel that you've missed out on taste when you try this easy-to-make Peppered Ahi Tuna with Greens! The tuna in this recipe is deliciously meaty—since it's left raw in the middle and seared on the edges—and its buttery flavor is irresistible, especially when coated with a thin layer of peppery spices. If you want to add an extra layer of spicy flavor, top this succulent salad with a little wasabi for an added kick.

Serves 4

For Vinaigrette:
¾ cup balsamic vinegar
Juice of 1 orange
1 teaspoon orange zest

For Peppered Ahi Tuna:
1 pound ahi tuna fillet
1 teaspoon sea salt
1 teaspoon ground coriander
1 teaspoon paprika
½ teaspoon garlic powder
¼ teaspoon cayenne pepper
2 tablespoons ground pepper
   (large grounds)
2 tablespoons coconut oil
8 cups salad greens
4 lemon wedges, for garnish
   (optional)

1. **For Vinaigrette:** In a small sauce pot, combine balsamic vinegar, orange juice, and zest and bring to a boil. Turn heat down to low and simmer until the mixture starts to thicken, about 5 minutes. Refrigerate until ready to serve.

2. **For Peppered Ahi Tuna:** Using a thin, sharp knife, cut the fillet into 4 equal size steaks. Combine salt, coriander, paprika, garlic powder, cayenne pepper, and ground pepper in a small bowl and whisk until blended. Pour spices onto a plate. Take each tuna steak and roll in the spices. Press down gently on each side to make sure the tuna is encrusted, but be cautious to avoid bruising the fish.

3. Heat coconut oil in a large skillet over medium-high to high heat. Once the coconut oil is liquefied and the skillet is hot, sear the tuna steaks for about 1 minute per side, until both are done. Remove steaks from heat, place on a cutting board, and let rest 1 minute.

4. Evenly slice each tuna steak into about 5 diagonal slices (or more depending on desired thinness of each slice), and place atop 2 cups of salad greens. Drizzle with vinaigrette and garnish with a lemon wedge, if desired.

Spicy Chicken Salad

Nothing is better than a crunchy piece of endive lettuce filled with a meaty and flavorful chicken salad, and this spicy, Asian-infused version is nothing short of mouthwatering! The ginger and Sriracha sauce really pack a punch in this mixture. This recipe is also a great way to use up leftover chicken breasts or roasted chicken! If you have a sweet tooth, adding grapes and nuts to this recipe will add a bit of sweet crunch to your spice.

1. Preheat oven to 350°F.

2. Sprinkle chicken breasts with salt and pepper and place on a foil-lined baking sheet, sprayed with nonstick spray. Bake for 30 minutes, until cooked through. Remove chicken from oven and chill in refrigerator.

3. Once chilled, shred the chicken with your hands. Place shredded chicken in a medium mixing bowl with remaining ingredients (except for the lettuce). Fold ingredients together until blended. Serve scooped into endive lettuce leaves.

Serves 3

1 pound chicken breasts (about 3 large breasts)
Pinch salt and pepper
½ cup Paleo Mayo (see recipe in Chapter 5)
1½ tablespoons Sriracha sauce
1 tablespoon freshly chopped cilantro
½ teaspoon freshly grated ginger
½ cup finely chopped celery
1 green onion, thinly sliced
1 head endive lettuce

🌶 SRIRACHA STATS

Sriracha is a hot sauce originating from the city of Si Racha, Thailand. It is a smooth chili pepper and garlic paste, and is frequently used in American-based Thai cuisine for spice. In its native home of Thailand, Sriracha is often used as a dipping sauce. It can be found in the multicultural section of most major grocery stores.

Zesty Mandarin Salad with Ginger Vinaigrette

Ginger, spice, and everything nice is what this Zesty Mandarin Salad with Ginger Vinaigrette is made of! The delicious Asian-infused dressing elegantly coats the sweet and refreshing citrus salad. The ginger provides the zest and thickens the dressing quite a bit. This vinaigrette is a great accompaniment to any salad or slaw! It can also be used as a marinade or dipping sauce for grilled chicken or steak.

Yields 1 cup

For Ginger Vinaigrette:
½ cup extra-virgin olive oil
¼ cup champagne vinegar
¼ cup Dijon mustard
2 tablespoons freshly grated ginger
½ teaspoon raw organic honey
½ teaspoon dried parsley
½ teaspoon sea salt
½ teaspoon pepper
Pinch cayenne pepper

For Zesty Mandarin Salad:
3–4 cups field greens
½ cup mandarin oranges
¼ cup almond slices

1. **For Ginger Vinaigrette:** Place all ingredients in a small mixing bowl and mix with an immersion blender (or whisk) until well blended and frothy. Store in an airtight container and shake well before each use.

2. **For Zesty Mandarin Salad:** Toss the field greens, oranges, and almonds together gently in a medium salad bowl and drizzle with 2–3 tablespoons of the Ginger Vinaigrette.

♨ MANDARIN SALAD

This zesty vinaigrette pairs perfectly with a simple citrus salad. Consider using a mix of field greens, a generous portion of mandarin oranges, and thick slices of almond. The simple, fresh nature of the salad perfectly accentuates this super-flavorful dressing. Add a pinch of crushed red pepper flakes to heat up the intensity!

Tasty Thai Beef Salad

This refreshing spicy salad is everything you would expect—and more. The marinade gives the steak a deep, garlicky flavor that will set your tongue a-tingle! When placed on top of a light summery salad, this steak is the perfect way to entice the palate. Try it as a main course too, with sautéed snap peas as a side!

1. **For Steak:** Combine coconut aminos, lime juice and zest, garlic, fresh basil, and red pepper flakes into a quart-size sealable freezer bag. Mix ingredients together lightly. Add steak to bag, and marinate in the refrigerator for at least 1 hour (overnight is best, as the flavors have a chance to really mesh together). Preheat grill to medium heat. Once heated, grill the steak for about 5 minutes per side for medium/medium-rare temperature. (Keep on the heat longer for a more well-done steak.) Let the steak sit on a cutting board to rest, about 5–10 minutes.

2. **For Salad:** While the steak is resting, combine the chopped salad vegetables in a mixing bowl, and divide onto 2 plates. Slice steak into thin ½" slices and place on top of salads. Drizzle each with 2 tablespoons of the Spicy Thai Dressing and ½ teaspoon fresh basil leaves.

Serves 2

For Steak:
¼ cup coconut aminos
Juice and zest of 1 lime
2 cloves garlic, peeled and halved
1 tablespoon freshly chopped basil
1 teaspoon dried red pepper flakes
½ pound sirloin

For Salad:
¼ head cabbage, finely chopped
¼ head iceberg lettuce, finely chopped
1 large carrot, peeled and chopped into matchsticks
1 bell pepper, chopped into matchsticks
¼ cup of Spicy Thai Dressing (recipe in this chapter)
½ teaspoon fresh basil leaves

Spicy Thai Dressing over Bok Choy Slaw

This cool, refreshing vegetable salad is a perfect canvas for the Spicy Thai Dressing! The salty flavor from the anchovy paste combined with the spice from the cayenne pepper and lime zest will light up your taste buds. This dish is perfect when served with grilled salmon or steak on a cool summer night, and is an excellent lunch option as well.

Serves 3–4

For Spicy Thai Dressing:
½ cup extra-virgin olive oil
¼ cup rice wine vinegar
1 teaspoon sesame oil
¼ teaspoon anchovy paste
Juice and zest of 1 lime
½ teaspoon dried basil
Pinch cayenne pepper
Sea salt and pepper, to taste

For Bok Choy Salad:
4 baby bok choy, washed and
    thinly sliced
1 carrot, peeled and sliced into
    thin rounds
2 celery stalks, thinly sliced
½ cucumber, thinly sliced

1. **For Spicy Thai Dressing:** Place all ingredients in a small mixing bowl and mix with an immersion blender (or whisk) until well blended and frothy.

2. **For Bok Choy Salad:** Gently toss the bok choy, carrot, celery, and cucumber together in a large bowl, and then divide evenly onto 2 separate serving plates and drizzle each with 2–3 tablespoons of the Spicy Thai Dressing. Store unused dressing in an airtight container and shake well before each use.

Fiery Fiesta Salad Wraps

How does spicy, juicy ground turkey wrapped in crisp iceberg lettuce sound to you? Mouthwatering, of course! These Fiery Fiesta Salad Wraps are a healthy lunch or dinner option that will tantalize the senses. Feel free to use other types of meat with this recipe, like ground beef or chicken.

1. Add lean turkey to a skillet over medium heat, breaking up into pieces as it cooks. Drain excess fat from the turkey once cooked half-way through. Add spices to the turkey, stir to combine, and cook completely. Remove turkey from the skillet and place in a covered dish.

2. In the same skillet, over medium-high heat, add olive oil. Sauté onion and bell pepper until they start to blacken (press down into the pan to help this process), then remove from heat.

3. To create salad wraps, add a scoop of spicy turkey meat to a whole leaf of iceberg let-tuce. Top with sautéed onions and peppers, sprinkle of chopped jalapeño, a few chunks of avocado, and a scoop of salsa. Wrap lettuce around filling and enjoy.

Serves 2–3

½ pound ground turkey meat
1 teaspoon paprika
1 teaspoon cumin
1 teaspoon chili powder
1 teaspoon garlic powder
1 teaspoon pepper
¼ teaspoon cayenne pepper
    (add more if you like it hot!)
1 tablespoon olive oil
½ medium onion, sliced
1 bell pepper, julienned
1 head iceberg lettuce
    (separated into whole leaves,
    rinsed)
1 jalapeño, seeded and chopped
½ avocado, pitted and peeled
Salsa, to taste

Spicy Tuna Salad

This simple tuna salad is the perfect way to top off a bed of dark leafy greens. The powerful paprika and pepper combination create an intense degree of spice! Adjust the heat by increasing or decreasing the amount of cayenne pepper used. For the really daring, add a finely chopped jalapeño and prepare the fire extinguisher!

Serves 2–3

2 (5-ounce) cans white albacore tuna packed in water, drained
2 celery stalks, diced
2 tablespoons diced red onion
1 medium dill pickle, diced
2–3 tablespoons Paleo Mayo (see Chapter 5)
1 teaspoon Dijon mustard
½ teaspoon celery salt
½ teaspoon pepper
¼ teaspoon cayenne pepper
¼ teaspoon paprika
4–6 cups salad greens
1–2 teaspoons each, of olive oil and lemon juice
Salt and pepper to taste

Shred tuna and add to mixing bowl with all other ingredients except greens, olive oil, and lemon juice. Fold together with a fork. Serve over a bed of greens, drizzle with olive oil and lemon juice, and sprinkle with salt and pepper to taste.

Spicy Sweet Potato Salad

The flavors found in this Spicy Sweet Potato Salad are a magnificent harmony of sweet, spicy, and savory. There is room for so much versatility here, so let your creativity run wild! Experiment with additional spices like chipotle pepper, hot sauce, and more, and vary the veggies as well. Try adding some beets for color, or chopped asparagus for crunch!

1. In a large bowl, mix Paleo Mayo and mustard. Add sweet potatoes, cumin, red pepper flakes, celery, red bell pepper, pineapple, green onions, and jalapeños, and toss gently.

2. Season to taste with salt and pepper. Cover and refrigerate about 1 hour. Fold in pecans and sprinkle with chives.

Serves 8

¼ cup Paleo Mayo (see Chapter 5)
1 tablespoon mustard
4 small sweet potatoes, cooked, peeled, and cubed
1 teaspoon cumin
1 teaspoon red pepper flakes
4 large celery stalks, sliced ¼" thick
1 red bell pepper, diced
1 cup diced fresh pineapple
2 green onions, finely chopped
2 jalapeños, finely chopped
Salt and pepper, to taste
½ cup coarsely chopped pecans, toasted
2–3 tablespoons chopped fresh chives

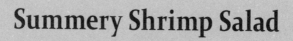

Summery Shrimp Salad

This summery chopped seafood salad is a cool and refreshing lunch option! It is super easy to make and requires barely any time in the kitchen. The Dijon mustard and jalapeños add a spicy mix to this salad, and create a harmony of flavors with the honey and citrus tones in the vinaigrette mixture. This hot and spicy salad is packed with protein—and it's sure to be a fulfilling meal!

Serves 2–3

3 eggs, hard boiled, peeled, and chopped

2 cups cooked and peeled shrimp, chopped

1 green apple, cored and diced

½ red onion, diced

4 celery stalks, diced

2–3 jalapeños, sliced

¼ cup ground Dijon mustard

2 tablespoons lemon juice

1 tablespoon olive oil

1 tablespoon raw organic honey

1 tablespoon cilantro

1 teaspoon chipotle pepper

½ teaspoon parsley

½ teaspoon thyme

½ teaspoon basil

Salt and pepper, to taste

Place eggs, shrimp, apple, onion, and celery in a large bowl. Add all the remaining ingredients to the bowl and mix well. Chill and serve.

Essenced Egg Salad

Egg salad is definitely a comfort food, and just a small amount will fill you up. This spicy Paleo version is sure to please! The spice in this recipe is not overbearing, but extra heat can always be added to make this a fiery lunch option. This is great on top of a salad. Try adding chopped vegetables if you like crunch! Celery, onions, jalapeños, and other vegetables work well.

Peel cooled eggs and roughly chop. Place in a bowl and add all other ingredients. Mash/fold ingredients with a fork until well blended. Serve chilled.

Serves 2

6 large eggs, boiled and cooled
1½ tablespoons Paleo Mayo
    (see Chapter 5)
1 teaspoon Dijon mustard
½ teaspoon garlic powder
½ teaspoon paprika
¼ teaspoon cayenne pepper
2 chives, chopped
Salt and pepper, to taste

Crazy Crab Salad in Avocado Bowls

This crazy crab salad can be enjoyed any time of year—it is very versatile! This flavorful salad pairs wonderfully with the creaminess of the avocado, and the green onions, cumin, onion, and peppers kick up the excitement! If you do not have Paleo Mayo on hand, double up on the Dijon mustard. This adds an extra zing and is lower in fat and calories.

Yields 4 individual avocado bowls

1 cup lump crab meat
1 tablespoon Paleo Mayo (see Chapter 5)
1 tablespoon Dijon mustard
1 tablespoon chopped red onion
1 teaspoon chopped jalapeño
¼ teaspoon ground cumin
Juice of ½ lime
Pinch sea salt and black pepper, or more to taste
2 avocados, halved and pitted
1 green onion, chopped

Mix all ingredients (except for the avocados and green onion) in a medium mixing bowl. Spoon ¼ cup of mixture into each halved avocado. Top with chopped green onion, if desired.

Spicy Salmon Salad

This Spicy Salmon Salad is a great change of pace from the common lunch option, tuna salad. The salmon adds a deeper, fishier flavor, and the chopped cucumber and avocado offer a cool, creamy taste that's perfect against the zing of the Tabasco. This satisfying meal is also packed with protein, vitamins, minerals, and heart-healthy omega-3 fatty acids. What's not to love?

1. In a medium mixing bowl, combine salmon, mayo, Tabasco sauce, paprika, dill, green onion, cucumber, and avocado. With a fork, mix ingredients together until blended.

2. Serve cold over a bed of romaine. Sprinkle with salt and pepper.

Serves 2

½ pound cooked salmon, cold
½ cup Paleo Mayo (see Chapter 5)
½ teaspoon Tabasco sauce
½ teaspoon paprika
¼ teaspoon dried dill
1 green onion, sliced into thin rounds
1 cucumber, chopped into bite-size pieces
1 avocado, peeled, pitted, and diced
4 cups of chopped romaine lettuce
Salt and pepper, to taste

Chipotle Tomato Sauce

Try this southwestern take on the classic Italian tomato sauce on a Paleo pasta dish, or use it as a salsa on a southwestern dish of choice. The chipotle peppers and fresh cilantro create a super spiced-up sauce that is sure to make your eyes water!

Serves 6

3 cloves garlic, minced

1 large onion, minced

1 (28-ounce) can crushed
   tomatoes

1 (14-ounce) can diced
   tomatoes

3 chipotle peppers in adobo,
   minced

1 teaspoon dried oregano

1 tablespoon fresh cilantro,
   minced

½ teaspoon freshly ground
   black pepper

Place all the ingredients into a 4-quart slow cooker. Cook on low for 8–10 hours. Stir before serving.

🔥 KNOW YOUR SLOW COOKER

When using a new or new-to-you slow cooker for the first time, pick a day when someone can be there to keep tabs on it. In general, older slow cookers cook at a higher temperature than new models, but even new slow cookers can have some differences. It is a good idea to know the quirks of a particular slow cooker so food is not overcooked or undercooked. Tweak cooking times accordingly.

Jalapeño Tomatillo Sauce

Serve this spicy sauce over a fiery southwestern dish to really pump up the heat. The jalapeños and tomatillos create a tasty verde sauce, and the spice really sneaks up on you! But even though this dish is hot, there is always room for more, so experiment with chili peppers, hot sauce, or cayenne pepper for an even more powerful punch!

1. Heat the oil in a nonstick pan over medium heat. Sauté the garlic, onion, tomatillos, and jalapeños for 5–10 minutes, until softened.

2. Place the mixture into a 4-quart slow cooker. Add the water and stir. Cook on low for 8 hours.

Serves 4

1 teaspoon canola oil
2 cloves garlic, minced
1 medium onion, sliced
7 large tomatillos, diced
2 jalapeños, minced
½ cup water

🔥 TOMATO, TOMAHTO, OR TOMATILLO!

Tomatillos are essentially green cherry tomatoes. They are members of the nightshade family, which also include red tomatoes, white potatoes, eggplant, and all varieties of peppers. Frequently used in Mexican cuisine, tomatillos grow within husks that are inedible, and should be removed before consumption. The tastes of tomatillos are quite variable and range from sour to mild and sweet.

Cilantro Citrus Lettuce Wraps

These perfect healthy little snacks pack spice and crunch into every bite! While the citrus and cilantro create an amazing melody in your mouth—especially when they're combined with the heat from the chili sauce—the ginger and honey are settling and sweet. Enjoy inside wraps of lettuce as seen here, or cut and serve on toothpicks as hors d'oeuvres.

Serves 4–6

1 tablespoon olive oil
½ cup chopped yellow onion
1 cup chopped mushrooms
1 cup chopped cashews
1 tablespoon garlic
1 pound ground chicken
2 tablespoons Sriracha sauce
1 tablespoon raw organic honey
6 large iceberg lettuce leaves

1. In a large sauté pan, heat olive oil over medium heat. Add chopped onion and sauté for 5 minutes, or until translucent. Add mushrooms, cashews, and garlic and sauté for 3–4 more minutes. Push everything in the pan to the sides and add ground chicken to the center. Cook until chicken is cooked through and crumbly.

2. Add the Sriracha sauce and honey to the meat and stir until ingredients are well blended. Scoop ½ cup (or more) of the contents from the pan, to a lettuce leaf, wrap and enjoy! Repeat with remaining iceberg lettuce leaves, until all the pan's contents are used up.

🔥 FILL 'ER UP!

These lettuce wraps can be filled with any type of mixture. Try making them with shredded lamb, onion, and cilantro for a dinner entrée, or with scrambled eggs and smoked salmon for breakfast. Wrap your next turkey "sandwich" for tomorrow's lunch, for a quick and easy Paleo lunch box favorite!

Cold Cucumber Noodles with a Kick

In this recipe, the combination of cool cucumber is perfectly accented with a touch of heat and sweet. This is a healthy and satisfying option for a side to any main dish, and is great as a small salad too. However, it is best enjoyed in the summer as a cool snack, when cucumbers are at their best! The "kick" in this dish is from the fiery Sriracha and red pepper duo—a titillating twosome—so get your taste buds ready!

1. Slice the cucumber in half the long way. Using a mandoline, slice the cucumber halves into thin, ¼"-thick strips. Cut these strips the long way, into cucumber "noodles."

2. Whisk all other ingredients in a medium bowl and add cucumber. Stir until all cucumber pieces are covered with mixture.

Serves 2

1 large English seedless cucumber
½ tablespoon olive oil
1 teaspoon rice wine vinegar
Pinch red pepper flakes
1 teaspoon raw organic honey
½ teaspoon Sriracha sauce
½ teaspoon garlic powder
Pinch salt and pepper

Seaweed Salad

Seaweed salad is a great accompaniment to fish dishes, especially raw fish (as in sushi). The crunch and saltiness of seaweed is something you will crave over and over again, and this version is seasoned to really capture that rich, briny flavor, but with an added kick. If you're looking for an even hotter dish, try adding a pinch of wasabi powder to this recipe to get a deeper, more pungent heat.

Serves 2

3 tablespoons rice vinegar
2 tablespoons coconut aminos
1 tablespoon sesame oil
¾ teaspoon raw organic honey
¼ teaspoon Sriracha sauce
1 teaspoon red pepper flakes
1 teaspoon freshly grated ginger
½ teaspoon minced garlic
1 ounce wakame seaweed
1 tablespoon white and black sesame seed mix, preferably toasted

1. In a small sauce pot, combine all ingredients (except for the seaweed and sesame seeds). Heat over medium heat and whisk occasionally. Heat for about 5 minutes, so flavors are able to meld. Place in refrigerator to cool.

2. Soak seaweed in warm water, making sure it is fully submerged, for about 6 minutes. Drain and rinse under cool water. Squeeze out any excess water. Cut into strips approximately ½" wide.

3. Add seaweed to the gingery mixture and stir. Stir in sesame seeds and enjoy!

♨ EAT YOUR SEA VEGGIES!

Seaweed is an ancient sea vegetable that contains ample amounts of minerals and nutrients, and has been a part of Asian cuisine for centuries. Not only does it help boost immunity against illness and give you increased brain health, but the amount of iodine, calcium, and fiber it contains may help give you a healthier digestive system, faster metabolism, and healthier hair and nails! This rare ingredient is delicious with raw fish and other seafood dishes, but it can also be incorporated in other dishes. Try it in your favorite stir fry dish or lettuce wrap, or as a salad topping!

Spicy Green Hummus

This light, Middle Eastern–inspired Paleo version of hummus is irresistible! The creamy avocados are perfectly offset by the pungent tahini and spicy cayenne pepper. Try adding roasted red peppers, roasted garlic, and other savory vegetables for added flavor and texture! This green hummus can be used as a spread, dip, or salad topping.

1. Spoon out avocado flesh from the peels.

2. Add avocado and all other ingredients to a food processor. Blend on low for about 2 minutes, until smooth and there are no large chunks of avocado left. Add more olive oil if the mixture is too pasty. Remove from food processor and serve.

🔥 AVOCAD-OH!

To core an avocado, use a sharp knife to slice evenly all the way around the length of the fruit. You will feel a large seed in the middle. Once you have sliced your knife all the way around, twist both sides apart and pull. Your avocado should pull apart into two even sections. Discard the large black pit in the center, scoop out the avocado flesh with a spoon, and enjoy!

Serves 8–10

4 ripe avocados, halved and pitted
2 tablespoons lemon juice (about ½ lemon squeezed)
3 teaspoons minced garlic (about 3 cloves)
1 tablespoon olive oil
1 tablespoon tahini
½ teaspoon cumin
¼ teaspoon cayenne pepper
Sea salt and pepper, to taste

Spicy Skewered Shrimp with Pineapple

This spicy, summery dish is delicious when grilled or if you're looking to add some extra heat to a hot summer day. Shrimp do not take long to cook at all, and skewers allow for an easy cleanup, so this dish is an easy meal for those hot, humid days when you don't feel like spending a lot of time in the kitchen. The Homemade Cajun Seasoning can be adjusted to any desired spiciness by adding (or reducing) the amounts of cayenne pepper and paprika used. This mix is also great on steak, chicken, and other seafood!

Serves 4–6

For Homemade Cajun Seasoning:

1 teaspoon paprika
1 teaspoon garlic powder
1 teaspoon sea salt
½ teaspoon black pepper
½ teaspoon onion powder
½ teaspoon cayenne pepper
½ teaspoon oregano
½ teaspoon thyme
½ teaspoon red pepper flakes

For Spicy Skewered Shrimp with Pineapple:

10–12 skewers, soaked in water
2 pounds large shrimp, peeled and deveined (about 30–40 shrimp)
Juice of 1 lemon (about 3–4 teaspoons)
2 tablespoons Homemade Cajun Seasoning
1 pineapple, chopped into bite-size chunks
3 tablespoons olive oil
Lemon wedges, for garnish

1. **For Homemade Cajun Seasoning:** Add all ingredients to a mortar and pestle and grind to a fine, sand-like consistency. Transfer to a large zip-top bag and set aside.

2. **For Spicy Skewered Shrimp with Pineapple:** Soak skewers in water for about 1 hour before turning on grill. In a mixing bowl, combine shrimp and lemon juice. Add the shrimp to the zip-top bag with the Homemade Cajun Seasoning, and shake lightly to coat. Remove from bag and place onto skewers, alternating shrimp and pineapple; 4–5 shrimp and pineapple chunks per skewer work best.

3. Coat grill grates with olive oil to prevent shrimp and pineapple from sticking. Preheat the grill to a medium flame and cook skewers for about 2–3 minutes per side, or until shrimp turn pink. Remove from heat and enjoy.

Indian Savory Spice Nuts

These Indian Savory Spice Nuts are finger-licking good and will be a hit at any party! The combination of garam masala, cumin, cardamom, and chili powder packs so many flavors into every bite. Garam masala is a traditional Indian seasoning made up of many different spices, like peppercorns, cloves, cinnamon, cumin, and cardamom. This deliciously spicy mixture can be found at your local grocery store.

1. Preheat the oven to 250°F.

2. Add nuts to a large mixing bowl and slowly mix with olive oil so all are evenly coated. Place the nuts on a baking sheet lined with parchment paper, and bake in the oven for about 45 minutes.

3. Mix all spices together in large bowl. Once nuts are done baking, transfer to bowl and mix with spices while warm.

Yields 3 cups

1 cup plain almonds
1 cup plain cashews
1 cup plain pecans
1 tablespoon olive oil
1½ teaspoons chili powder
1 teaspoon cumin
½ teaspoon ground cardamom
½ teaspoon garam masala
Sea salt and pepper, to taste

Devilish Deviled Eggs

These deviled eggs will be the first to go at any gathering, and they will be a special treat for the guests who enjoy a bit of added spice! The fiery flavor from the spicy mustard and cayenne accent the creaminess from the egg yolks and avocado deliciously, and the hot sauce provides a pop of tangy heat that is sure to excite any palate.

Serves 24

1 dozen large hard-boiled eggs, cooled and peeled
1 large avocado, pitted and peeled
2 tablespoons spicy mustard
2 tablespoons Paleo Mayo (see Chapter 5)
¼ teaspoon cayenne pepper
½ teaspoon paprika
Hot sauce, to taste (Tabasco works well)

1. Evenly slice eggs lengthwise and remove yolks.

2. Place yolks in a medium mixing bowl with avocado, spicy mustard, Paleo Mayo, and cayenne pepper. Mash together with a fork, and stir until well blended with a smooth consistency. Place mixture in a piping tube (or a plastic bag with a tip of the corner cut off to make a hole).

3. Place egg white halves on a serving plate/platter and fill each with the yolk mixture. Sprinkle each with paprika and a drop of hot sauce before serving.

Paleo Wild Wings

These juicy, succulent wings are sure to make you sweat; the crunchy skin of each wing is packed with layers of fiery flavor! The process of steaming and refrigerating the wings before baking actually draws out the moisture from the skin, creating a crispier layer of skin and juicier meat.

1. Preheat the oven to 425°F.

2. Steam wings in a double boiler for 10 minutes. (This trick partially cooks the wings.) Remove from boiler and place neatly on a flat roasting rack on a large baking sheet. Pat dry with a paper towel and refrigerate for 1 hour.

3. Sprinkle the salt, pepper, garlic powder, and cayenne pepper mixture over all of the wings, then bake for 20 minutes, flipping wings over halfway through.

4. While the wings are baking, combine hot sauce, honey, spicy mustard, and clarified butter in a small sauce pot on medium heat. Whisk until all ingredients are combined and smooth.

5. Remove wings from oven and use a basting brush to coat wings with the hot sauce mixture. Serve hot alongside celery and carrot sticks.

Serves 3–6

12 chicken wings
½ teaspoon each of salt, pepper, garlic powder, and cayenne pepper, combined
½ cup Frank's Red Hot sauce
¼ cup raw organic honey
¼ cup spicy mustard
2 tablespoons clarified butter
3–6 celery sticks
3–6 carrot sticks

🔥 CLARIFIED BUTTER: WHY ALL THE HYPE?

Clarified butter and a similar product known as ghee, which is of Indian origin, are essentially forms of butter from which most of the water, sugar, and milk proteins (casein and whey) are removed. It is helpful to use when cooking at very high temperatures, since it is extremely heat stable, making burning very unlikely.

Sizzlin' Curry Grilled Beef Kabobs

Kabobs originate from the Middle East, and are now a delicious dinner option all over the world! These Sizzlin' Curry Grilled Beef Kabobs are full of flavor and are guaranteed to spice up your dinner. The turmeric and curry add a warm, peppery flavor and a bright yellow tint of color. This delicious marinade could work on other types of skewers as well. Try it with shrimp, chicken, or vegetables!

Serves 4–6

10–12 skewers, soaked in water
4 cloves garlic
⅓ cup red wine vinegar
1 teaspoon curry
1 teaspoon paprika
½ teaspoon turmeric
¼ teaspoon cayenne pepper
½ cup olive oil
2 pounds grass-fed sirloin
    steak, cut into thick strips
Heavy pinch sea salt and pepper

1. Soak wooden skewers in water for 1 hour before grilling.

2. Place garlic, vinegar, and spices into medium mixing bowl. Gradually incorporate olive oil while blending ingredients with immersion blender until garlic is chopped and well blended.

3. Place steak strips in a large plastic bag and coat with marinade. Refrigerate for at least 1 hour before grilling.

4. Remove steak strips from plastic bag after marinating and slide onto skewers. Preheat grill on medium to medium-high heat and grill kabobs for about 5 minutes per side. Remove from heat, add salt and pepper, and serve.

Zesty Carrot Dip

Carrots are a naturally sweet vegetable, so you'll achieve a flavorful medley when you add harissa to them! Harissa is a type of hot chili sauce that originated in Tunisia. It is typically made with a combination of hot chili peppers, serrano peppers, and garlic, and it adds a layer of spice to this dip. This recipe is great as a snack or vegetarian option and can be stored for up to 3 days before serving.

1. Place cut carrots in a medium sauce pot and fill with water until carrots are fully immersed. Boil for 15–20 minutes, or until carrots are soft, then remove from heat, drain water, and let cool slightly.

2. Add carrots to a food processor with garlic, lemon juice, harissa, cumin, paprika, parsley, salt, and pepper. Blend ingredients and slowly incorporate olive oil into processor.

3. Once all of the olive oil has been added, continue to pulse until you reach a smooth, puréed texture. Serve chilled with crudités.

Yields 1½ cups

1 pound carrots, peeled and cut into bite-size chunks

2 cloves garlic

2 tablespoons lemon juice

1 teaspoon Homemade Harissa (see Chapter 5)

1 teaspoon cumin

1 teaspoon paprika

1 teaspoon parsley

Salt and pepper, to taste

2 tablespoons olive oil

3–4 cups of an assortment of chilled raw veggies of choice (e.g., carrots, peppers, cucumbers, celery, cherry tomatoes, etc.)

🔥 SPICY BETA-CAROTENE

Beta-carotene, which gives carrots their orange pigment, is a naturally occurring, fat-soluble compound that can be converted to active vitamin A and retinol, an essential component in eye health. It is also beneficial for immune health, protecting against toxins, colds, flu, and infections. As an antioxidant, it helps defend against cellular breakdown.

Seasoned Sea Scallops Wrapped in Bacon

These Seasoned Sea Scallops Wrapped in Bacon are a zesty variation of a popular party food. There is no limit to the amount of spice you can add to these scallops, as they are a fairly sweet mollusk that can adapt to any flavor! Try wrapping the scallops in pepper-crusted bacon for added spice and crunch.

Yields 1 dozen

12 thick slices nitrate-free bacon
12 large sea scallops
1 teaspoon Homemade Cajun Seasoning (see recipe for Spicy Skewered Shrimp with Pineapple in this chapter)
1 tablespoon olive oil
1 lemon

1. Preheat the oven to 400°F.

2. Place bacon slices on a large parchment-lined baking sheet in a single layer (do not overlap). Bake for about 10 minutes, flipping bacon halfway through. Bacon should be only partially cooked, and still pliable. Remove from heat and allow to cool for a few minutes.

3. Coat sea scallops with Cajun seasoning, then wrap each scallop with a bacon slice and fasten with a toothpick.

4. In a large skillet, heat olive oil over medium to medium-high heat. Place bacon-wrapped scallops in the skillet and sear about 4–5 minutes per side, until scallop is cooked through and bacon is crispy. Remove from heat, then slice lemon and squeeze lemon juice over scallops to taste.

Bison Meatballs and Fiery Marinara

These melt-in-your-mouth meatballs are guaranteed to be a huge hit at your next party or family dinner! The simplicity of the bison meatballs is snazzed up with the fiery marinara to give you an appetizer or dinner option that is sure to spice up your life. Try these meatballs atop roasted spaghetti squash as a "spaghetti dinner" option!

1. **For Fiery Marinara:** In a medium stock pot, combine ground and crushed tomatoes, tomato paste, green pepper, basil, oregano, bay leaf, cayenne pepper, red pepper flakes, honey, salt, and pepper. Bring to a boil and immediately turn to low. Simmer for at least 45 minutes. The longer you simmer, the more the flavors will meld together.

2. **For Bison Meatballs:** While the sauce is simmering, combine bison meat, eggs, flaxmeal, parsley, garlic, salt, and pepper in a medium mixing bowl. Mix gently with hands (do not manipulate the meat too much, or the meatballs will be tough). Form meat into small 1-ounce meatballs. Heat olive oil in a large sauté pan over medium-high heat. Add meatballs and cook until they start to brown on one side (about 3–4 minutes). Roll to the other side and cook for another 3–4 minutes.

3. Remove meatballs and add to stock pot with sauce. Simmer for about 15 minutes. Place meatballs on a serving platter with toothpicks, and top with a spoonful of extra sauce. Top each with a sprig of parsley and serve with toothpicks.

Yields about 20 meatballs

For Fiery Marinara:
- 1 (28-ounce) can ground peeled tomatoes
- 1 (14-ounce) can fire-roasted crushed tomatoes
- 1 teaspoon tomato paste
- ½ green bell pepper, whole
- 1 tablespoon freshly chopped basil
- 1 tablespoon freshly chopped oregano
- 1 bay leaf
- ¼ teaspoon cayenne pepper
- 1 teaspoon crushed red pepper flakes
- 1 teaspoon raw organic honey
- Large pinch sea salt and pepper

For Bison Meatballs:
- 1 pound ground bison meat
- 2 eggs
- ¼ cup ground flaxmeal
- 2 tablespoons freshly chopped parsley
- ½ teaspoon minced garlic
- ½ teaspoon salt
- ½ teaspoon pepper
- 2 tablespoons olive oil
- Parsley sprigs, for garnish

Mean Green Guacamole

Originating in Mexico, guacamole is a deliciously healthy snack or appetizer. Guacamole's star ingredient is the avocado, which is a cool and creamy fruit that meshes perfectly with a bit of heat. When perfectly ripe, the avocado will have a little bit of give when squeezed. Enjoy this hot and spicy Mean Green Guacamole with fresh crudités, or as a replacement to a creamy condiment in your favorite Mexican-inspired dish!

Yields 1 cup

2 avocados, pitted and peeled
1 clove garlic, minced
1 small red onion, finely diced
1 jalapeño, seeded and finely diced
Juice of 1 lime
Tabasco sauce to taste
Salt and pepper, to taste
Chopped cilantro, to taste

Combine all ingredients in a medium bowl. Mash with a fork until ingredients are blended with large chunks of avocado throughout. Serve chilled.

Slow Cooker Southwestern Chicken Salad

This hot and spicy Slow Cooker Southwestern Chicken Salad is a super easy way to liven up plain old chicken breasts! The simplicity of this one-pot meal leaves with you with a great-smelling house and easy cleanup! Be creative and vary the vegetables in the recipe, or be bold and incorporate some hot chili peppers or jalapeños for added spice.

1. In a medium bowl, combine the salsa with the pepper, cumin, and chili powder.

2. Place the onion and peppers on the bottom of a 4-quart slow cooker. Place the chicken breasts on top of the onions and peppers. Cover the chicken with the salsa and tomatoes. Cook on low for 8 hours.

3. Shred the chicken with a fork inside the slow cooker, and stir everything together to combine. Serve over mixed salad greens garnished with avocado slices.

Serves 4

16-ounces Slow-Cooked Spicy Salsa (see recipe in Chapter 6)
1 teaspoon pepper
1 teaspoon cumin
1 teaspoon chili powder
1 large onion, peeled, halved, and sliced
1 cup frozen (or fresh) diced bell peppers
4 boneless, skinless chicken breasts
1 (14.5-ounce) can diced tomatoes
Mixed salad greens, to taste
Avocado slices, for garnish

Crazy Good Cauliflower Hummus

Cauliflower is a versatile vegetable that can be incorporated into many dishes and adapted to any flavor. In this recipe, the Sriracha sauce and roasted red pepper give this hummus a reddish hue and a powerful punch of flavor. This is enjoyed as a fresh, cold dip and is great with crudités!

Yields 1–1½ cups

2 large heads cauliflower
3–4 tablespoons olive oil, divided use
1 teaspoon cumin
Large pinch salt and pepper
1 teaspoon minced garlic
½ cup water
½ cup tahini
1 teaspoon Sriracha sauce
1 large roasted red pepper
Pinch red pepper flakes
Pinch cayenne pepper

1. Preheat oven to 350°F.

2. Cut cauliflower into large chunks. Toss on a foiled baking sheet with 1 tablespoon of olive oil, cumin, salt, and pepper. Bake for about 25 minutes, and remove from heat to cool.

3. Once cooled, combine all ingredients (aside from the olive oil) in a food processor. Pulse until you get a smooth paste, while slowly incorporating olive oil between pulses until desired consistency is reached. Remove from food processor and store in an airtight container in the refrigerator for up to one week. Serve cold.

Stuffed Jalapeños in a Bacon Blanket

You are sure to be the hit of any cocktail party if you arrive with these spicy little snacks! After all, who could resist something wrapped in bacon? These jalapeño poppers are super spicy, savory, and satisfying. The mixed, sautéed veggies are a delicious, no carbohydrate stuffing option that balance the heat of the fiery jalapeño to make this dish perfect for spice-lovers of varying degrees.

1. Preheat the oven to 375°F and line a baking sheet with foil. Add olive oil to a medium sauté pan over medium-high heat. Once heated, add onion and cook for about 5 minutes, or until translucent. Add cauliflower, garlic, and mushrooms, and season with salt and pepper. Continue sautéing for another 5 minutes, stirring occasionally, and then remove from heat.

2. Spoon the sautéed vegetable mixture into each hollow jalapeño pepper to the top. Wrap each pepper with a slice of bacon and seal with a toothpick. Bake the peppers for about 30 minutes, or until the bacon starts to crisp.

Yields 1 dozen

2 tablespoons olive oil
1 small onion, finely chopped
1 head cauliflower, grated (not including stems)
1 teaspoon minced garlic
1 (8-ounce) container mushrooms, chopped
Pinch salt and pepper
12 jalapeños (stems cut off and seeded; they should be hollow)
12 slices nitrate-free bacon

🔥 PEPPERS WITH PEP

There are many hot peppers out there, and it can be difficult to choose the right one! Here are the basics on popular peppers (often used in recipes) and how they measure on the Scoville Heat Index:

- *Bell pepper; Mild – 0*
- *Anaheim pepper; Mild/Medium – 1000–5000 (This would be a perfect, less spicy option for this recipe.)*
- *Jalapeño pepper; Medium – 2000–8000*
- *Cayenne pepper; Medium/Hot – 25000–50000*
- *Habanero pepper; Hot! – 150,000–350,000*

Spinach and Artichoke Dip with a Bacon Blaze

There is no denying that the creaminess of artichokes pairs beautifully with spinach. Even better, go ahead and enjoy some saltiness from bacon coupled with a little heat from Tabasco and cayenne pepper—an exciting enhancement to the already delicious duo! This fiery dip will surely be a hit amongst your heat-loving dinner guests.

Yields about 3 cups

8–10 slices peppered nitrate-free bacon

1 tablespoon olive oil

1 small onion, diced

1 tablespoon minced garlic

2½ cups fresh spinach

2 (14-ounce) cans artichoke hearts

1 tablespoon lemon juice

1 teaspoon Tabasco (2 if you want a lot of spice)

¼ teaspoon cayenne pepper

½ teaspoon salt and pepper

2 cups cashew cream

1 large tomato, diced

1. Preheat the oven to 375°F. Line bacon on a large foil-lined baking sheet. Bake for about 12 minutes, flipping bacon halfway through. Your bacon should be well done and crispy. Break apart into small bits. Leave the oven on 375°F.

2. In a large skillet, heat olive oil over medium heat. Add diced onion and sauté for about 10 minutes. Add garlic and spinach leaves and sauté until they wilt, no longer than 1–2 minutes. (You may have to add the spinach in batches.)

3. Add artichoke hearts, lemon juice, Tabasco sauce, cayenne pepper, salt, and pepper. Stir until ingredients are blended. Add bacon bits and cashew cream and stir together.

4. Pour mixture into an 8" × 8" baking dish, greased slightly with olive oil. Top with diced tomatoes and bake for 15 minutes, or until browned to a golden hue, watching carefully to avoid burning. Remove from heat and serve warm.

🔥 EAT YOUR VEGGIES!

Incorporate extra vegetables into this recipe for added texture, flavor, and nutrients. Sautéed zucchini and summer squash work perfectly with the spinach and artichokes, while extra diced tomatoes make a great topping! Turkey bacon or prosciutto can also replace the bacon in this recipe if you want to change up the taste.

Spicy Coconut Dipping Sauce

This creamy, peppery dipping sauce is absolutely perfect when served atop crudités, chicken, shrimp, or as a drizzle over a medley of cooked vegetables on your dinner plate. The heat in this Spicy Coconut Dipping Sauce comes from the notoriously potent Sriracha pepper, which will leave you looking for something to soothe that fiery tongue! For a more savory spice, add some Dijon mustard, and if you're looking for a thicker dipping sauce, just double the coconut yogurt and eliminate the coconut milk.

Mix almond butter and lime juice in a medium mixing bowl. Whisk in coconut milk. Mix in coconut yogurt, Sriracha sauce, and honey until well blended. Serve chilled as a dipping sauce.

Yields 1 cup

1 cup almond butter
Juice of 1 lime
¼ cup unsweetened coconut milk
¼ cup unsweetened coconut yogurt
¼ cup Sriracha sauce
1 teaspoon raw organic honey

Shrimp Cocktail with a Kick

Shrimp cocktail is always the first of the hors d'oeuvres to disappear! Why? The succulent shrimp is so crisp and refreshing to the palate, and the cocktail sauce kicks things up a notch and creates a lingering heat with each bite. The coolness of the chilled shrimp is ideal for softening the blow of the punch from the cayenne, horseradish, and Tabasco trio, so dig in and enjoy!

Yields approximately 2 dozen shrimp and 1 cup cocktail sauce

2 quarts water
2 tablespoons Old Bay Seasoning
¼ teaspoon cayenne pepper
Juice of 1 lemon, divided use
1 (1-pound) bag frozen, raw, uncooked large shrimp, peeled and deveined
¾ cup tomato purée
¼ cup tomato paste
¼ cup horseradish
Zest of ½ lemon
1 tablespoon Tabasco sauce

1. **For Shrimp:** Bring water to a boil in a large stock pot. Stir in Old Bay, cayenne pepper, and the juice from ½ lemon until well blended. Add in raw shrimp and turn down heat. Simmer for about 2 minutes, or until shrimp is opaque/pink and the edges just start to curl. Remove from heat, strain, and place on ice to halt the cooking process.

2. **For Cocktail Sauce:** In a medium mixing bowl, combine the leftover lemon juice, tomato purée, tomato paste, horseradish, lemon zest, and Tabasco sauce. Whisk until well blended and refrigerate along with the shrimp.

3. Best served chilled with shrimp displayed evenly on a large platter, around a small serving dish of cocktail sauce centered in the middle, with lemon slices to garnish.

Tantalizing Jalapeño "Tulips"

These Tantalizing Jalapeño Tulips hors d'oeuvres are as delicious as they are creative. It's a guarantee that they will be the most talked about dish at your next dinner party. The fiery jalapeños bring the zing, and the spices add the pep! In addition, the preparation is fun and is a great way for children to help in the kitchen. Enjoy!

1. Score (cut criss-crossing lines across the top) all the tomatoes, down about halfway.

2. Add chopped cucumber, almond yogurt, lime juice, chopped jalapeños, cilantro, garlic powder, salt, and pepper to a mixing bowl. Mix ingredients together. Stuff each tomato with this mixture and place them on their sides on a serving plate.

3. Stick 1 chive into the bottom of each tomato "tulip," to create stems, and serve chilled.

Yields 16 tulips

16 cherry tomatoes
⅓ of an English seedless cucumber, finely chopped
1½ cups plain unsweetened almond yogurt
Juice of ½ lime
2 jalapeños, seeded and finely chopped
2 tablespoons chopped cilantro
½ teaspoon garlic powder
½ teaspoon salt and pepper
16 chives

🔥 ADD PROTEIN TO THE PETALS!

Try stuffing these tart tomatoes with chilled seafood filling like the Crazy Crab Salad in Avocado Bowls or Spicy Tuna Salad (recipes found in this chapter). The Spicy Salmon Salad or the Spicy Chicken Salad (recipes found in this chapter) would also suffice! Still not satisfied? Try using some spiced-up ground beef or bison.

Hot and Naughty Tomatoes

These Hot and Naughty Tomatoes make a perfect quick and light snack or appetizer for any summer night! These can be enjoyed as a side, on a skewer, or as a salad topper. Feel free to try different types of tomatoes in this recipe (grape, plum, and many more!) or add other vegetables (like shallots or spinach) to complete this side dish. The Sriracha creates the heat in this recipe, and there is a lot of room for versatility here. Try this recipe with double the amount of Sriracha and add some cumin and hot pepper to really intensify the spice!

Serves 4

4 large tomatoes
2 tablespoons olive oil
¼ cup white wine vinegar
¼ teaspoon minced garlic
1 teaspoon Sriracha sauce
¼ teaspoon ground ginger
Pinch salt and pepper
1 teaspoon clarified butter
1 green onion, finely chopped,
   for garnish

1. Cut tomatoes, from the stem side down, into four large slices. Place flat on a large plate and set aside.

2. Add olive oil, vinegar, garlic, Sriracha, ginger, salt, and pepper to a mixing bowl. Whisk vigorously until mixed well and frothy. Pour evenly over tomatoes on a plate. Turn tomatoes over a few times to coat on either side. Let tomatoes sit in marinade for a few minutes to absorb.

3. Melt the clarified butter in a large skillet over medium-high to high heat. Add tomatoes so they lay flat in the pan. (Cook in batches if necessary.) Sauté until the tomatoes start to brown and then flip. Wait until the bottoms brown, remove from heat, and serve hot. Garnish with green onion, if desired.

🔥 TOSS IT UP

The vinaigrette/marinade mixture in this recipe pairs perfectly with many vegetables, not just tomatoes. Try slathering it over some pepper, onion, and mushroom skewers before grilling, or eliminate the clarified butter and use it as a salad dressing. Experiment further and use it as a marinade on your next beef, fish, or poultry dish.

Peppery Bacon–Wrapped Apricots

These appetizers have a great blend of sweet and savory flavors, and spice! The Dijon mustard and honey blend into each little bite and pack a ton of flavor. After all, who could resist a crunchy, juicy, sweet apricot wrapped in a slice of peppery bacon? These Peppery Bacon–Wrapped Apricots are really easy to make and are perfect when served with a toothpick.

1. Preheat the oven to 350°F.

2. In a large skillet, partially cook the bacon on medium heat, until slightly cooked and not at all crispy. Wrap halved bacon strips around each apricot and fasten with a toothpick.

3. Whisk together honey and Dijon mustard until well blended and smooth. Remove a small amount of marinade; place in a smaller, separate bowl; and set aside. Using a marinade brush, coat each bacon-wrapped apricot with the honey mustard mixture from the larger bowl.

4. Bake the apricots for about 20 minutes, or until the bacon starts to crisp. Coat with the honey Dijon from the smaller bowl that was previously set aside, for added flavor before serving.

Yields 18

9 slices peppered nitrate-free bacon, halved
18 dried apricots
18 long toothpicks
¼ cup raw organic honey
¼ cup Dijon mustard

Tasty Tuna Tartare

Tuna tartare is a refreshing, zesty way of eating raw fish, and you'll love the fire in this hot and spicy dish. The wasabi powder and Sriracha work together to add a ton of spice to this tuna, which is then perfectly accented with Dijon mustard and lime juice. This tuna will melt in your mouth, and you will definitely go back for more! Serve individually as an appetizer or in a communal bowl with endive lettuce as a way of scooping up this delicious concoction.

Serves 2–3

½ pound fresh tuna steak, gently sliced into small bite-size cubes
½ cucumber, seeded and sliced into small cubes
1 avocado, peeled, pitted, and sliced into small cubes
1 jalapeño, seeded and sliced into small cubes
1 teaspoon olive oil
Juice of 1 lime
1 teaspoon coconut aminos
1 teaspoon Sriracha sauce
½ teaspoon raw organic honey
½ teaspoon Dijon mustard
½ teaspoon wasabi powder
Pinch red pepper flakes
Pinch salt and pepper
Toasted sesame seeds, for garnish (optional)

1. Combine cubes of tuna, cucumber, avocado, and jalapeño in a medium bowl.

2. In a smaller bowl, whisk together all other ingredients until well blended and frothy.

3. Carefully add the marinade to the cubed tuna and vegetables, folding in gently as to avoid ruining the shape of the avocado.

4. Serve as an appetizer or side dish. Garnish with sesame seeds, if desired.

🔥 FISHY, FISHY!

Try experimenting with other types of tender fish in place of tuna. A fresh pink sushi-grade salmon is a succulent and healthy replacement, as it is high in omega-3. If you are not a fan of raw seafood, try cooked crab or shrimp instead. If you are feeling really brave, try cubes of Grade A steak for a steak tartare!

Caliente Calamari

Originating in the Mediterranean, fried squid is a popular appetizer around the world. It's a great option if you're looking for a different type of protein to incorporate into a meal, and it's also high in antioxidants and vitamin B12. This is a deliciously spiced-up, healthier Paleo version of the typical fried calamari, and it tastes great as an appetizer on skewers or as a salad topper!

1. In a serving bowl, whisk together the olive oil, lemon juice, cumin, cayenne, and salt. Then stir in the garlic, red pepper, and dried oregano.

2. Preheat grill to medium-high heat, and once the grates are hot, char the squid for 1 minute on each side. Remove the squid from the grill, and slice (crosswise) into ¼"-thick rings, including the tendrils. Add squid to the prepared spicy lemon sauce, and sprinkle with black pepper. Serve hot.

Serves 6–8

¼ cup olive oil
1½ tablespoons lemon juice
½ teaspoon cumin
½ teaspoon cayenne pepper
½ teaspoon salt
1 clove garlic, thinly sliced
1 teaspoon crushed red pepper
½ teaspoon dried oregano
1 pound fresh squid, cleaned, rinsed, and well dried
Ground black pepper, to taste

Szechuan Salmon-Stuffed Mushrooms

Mushrooms are healthy, tasty vegetables that make a great addition to any meal! Their meaty flavor adds a deep, rich taste to this spicy Paleo dish. The spice from the hot sauce and five-spice powder really kick up this dish and bring together the flavors of the creamy salmon, Paleo Mayo mixture, and portobello mushrooms. If you're looking to turn this hors d'oeuvre into a filling dinner, just add the ingredients to a large portobello cap instead!

Serves 8–12

16–20 large portobello mushrooms, stems removed and chopped

3–4 green onions, chopped

1 large red bell pepper

1 large green bell pepper

2 tablespoons hot sauce

1 teaspoon chipotle pepper

1 teaspoon five-spice powder (cinnamon, fennel, cloves, star anise, white pepper)

1 tablespoon olive oil

1 (14-ounce) can salmon

8 ounces almond meal

Paleo Mayo (see Chapter 5), to moisten

1. Combine the mushroom stems, green onions, peppers, hot sauce, chipotle pepper, and five-spice powder in a bowl, and then transfer to a large frying pan coated with the 1 tablespoon of olive oil, and sauté over medium-low heat. During the last few minutes of sautéing, add the canned salmon, being careful not to overcook. Once cooked, remove from heat, and mix the spicy salmon mixture with almond meal and enough Paleo Mayo to hold the mixture together.

2. Place the portobello caps in a baking dish, fill with salmon mixture, cover, and chill. These can be made a day ahead. When preparing to serve, preheat the oven to 450°F and bake for 10–12 minutes.

CHAPTER 3

Soups, Stews, and Chilis

Soup, stew, and chili are the ultimate comfort foods. There is nothing better than a steaming, fragrant bowl of warm liquid hitting your stomach on a cold, dreary day—and it's even better if that warm bowl is filled with something hot and spicy. Throughout this chapter you'll find popular, everyday soups and stews, with a spiced-up Paleo twist!

Lamb, poultry, beef, and other sources of protein are featured in recipes like Texas Firehouse Chili, Sultry Lamb Stew, and Chicken Chili Verde that are hot in both temperature and flavor! In addition, a wide variety of hearty vegetables, fresh herbs, spices, and seasonings—like curry powder, cumin, and chipotle pepper—have all been incorporated.

In addition to being spicy and deliciously Paleo, one-pot meals are great for cleanup, and they allow for a medley of flavors to coalesce! It is super easy to throw a soup together with staple pantry ingredients and a few fresh vegetables. Consider making some of the soups, stews, and chili featured in this chapter in advance and freezing for later use. Recipes that are this hot, spicy, and easy-to-make are hard to resist!

Sultry Lamb Stew

Lamb is a delicate meat, but when combined with herbs and fiery spices, it can shock you with its flavor. As a red meat, lamb is an excellent source of zinc and iron, and due to its tenderness, it is also a perfect meat for stews. This hearty stew really captures the flavor of lamb, and it's perfectly seasoned—and spiced!

Serves 4–6

2 tablespoons olive oil
1 large onion, roughly chopped
2 large red bell peppers, roughly chopped
1 (16-ounce) container white mushrooms, roughly chopped
2 pounds lamb shoulder, cut into 2" cubes and seasoned with salt and pepper
1 (28-ounce) can diced fire-roasted tomatoes
2 tablespoons minced garlic
1 tablespoon rosemary
1 tablespoon paprika
1 teaspoon cayenne pepper
1 teaspoon red pepper flakes
1 bay leaf
2–3 (28-ounce) containers beef stock
Black pepper, to taste
Freshly cut parsley, to taste

1. Heat olive oil on medium to medium-high heat in a large Dutch oven. Once heated, add chopped onion and sauté until translucent, about 6–7 minutes.

2. Add chopped peppers and mushrooms and sauté for another 6–7 minutes until vegetables start to brown slightly. Remove to a separate bowl.

3. Add cubes of seasoned lamb to the stock pot and brown on all sides. You will start to see brown bits on the bottom of the pot. Scrape these to loosen, which will add flavor to your stew.

4. Add the vegetables back to the pot, and add diced tomatoes, garlic, spices, and bay leaf to the pot. Turn heat to high and stir ingredients for 1–2 minutes to incorporate flavors.

5. Add stock (up to 3 containers depending on how much liquid you prefer) and bring to a boil. Turn heat to low and simmer for 20 minutes before serving. Remove bay leaf. Sprinkle with black pepper and fresh cut parsley.

Peppery Pumpkin Bisque

This smooth, delicious soup incorporates sweet pumpkin with a spicy red chili pepper and zesty allspice! This Peppery Pumpkin Bisque is easy to make, and while the canned pumpkin makes this recipe super convenient, fresh pumpkin purée is always welcome as well! You can add to the spiciness of this dish by using additional peppers or other spices like cinnamon and cumin. This bisque can be enjoyed hot *or* cold, making it a convenient item to pack for lunch.

1. In a large sauce pot, sauté onion, garlic, and red chili pepper in olive oil over medium heat, until onions are translucent (about 10 minutes, stirring occasionally). Add pumpkin purée, chicken stock, salt, pepper, allspice, and honey. Bring mixture to a boil and turn heat to low. Simmer on low for 30–40 minutes. Remove from heat and let cool slightly.

2. Blend mixture with an immersion blender while still in the pot until completely smooth.

3. Place the pot back on medium heat and add coconut milk. Stir often and let simmer for 10 minutes. Remove from heat and sprinkle with nutmeg before serving.

Serves 4

1 large yellow onion, chopped
2 cloves garlic, chopped
1 small red chili pepper, chopped (or more to taste)
1 tablespoon olive oil
1 (16-ounce) can pumpkin purée
4 cups chicken stock
½ teaspoon sea salt
½ teaspoon black pepper
¼ teaspoon ground allspice
1 teaspoon raw organic honey
1 cup coconut milk
Grated nutmeg, to taste

Tasty Tomato Soup

With a warm and fiery flavor, courtesy of the Sriracha and red pepper flakes, this smooth tomato soup is perfect on a cold winter's day. The tart warmth of the fire-roasted tomatoes topped with sweet basil is a fantastic way to warm your body and soul! For an added creamy texture, top with avocado slices.

Serves 4–6

2 tablespoons olive oil
1 medium onion, roughly chopped
3 cloves garlic, roughly chopped
½ teaspoon salt and pepper
2 (28-ounce) cans plum tomatoes
2 cups chicken broth
1 tablespoon tomato paste
1 tablespoon Sriracha sauce
1 tablespoon raw organic honey
1 teaspoon dried basil
¼ teaspoon dried red pepper flakes
1 cup coconut milk
Basil sprigs, for garnish

1. In a large Dutch oven or stock pot, heat olive oil over medium heat. Once heated, add chopped onion, garlic, salt, and pepper and sauté until onions are translucent, about 5 minutes.

2. Add cans of plum tomatoes, chicken broth, tomato paste, Sriracha sauce, honey, dried basil, and red pepper flakes and simmer over medium-low heat for 10 minutes.

3. Use an immersion blender to mix all ingredients until you reach a smooth consistency. After it's blended, simmer for about 10 more minutes (if you want more spice, add more Sriracha during this step).

4. Add coconut milk and stir occasionally over low heat until ready to serve. Garnish with fresh basil sprigs.

🔥 LIKE YOUR LYCOPENE

Lycopene is an antioxidant compound that gives tomatoes and other fruits and vegetables their yellow, orange, and red color. Studies have shown it is a cancer-fighting agent that protects the body from harmful components called free radicals. This mineral is easily absorbed by eating raw and cooked tomatoes, as well as other fruits and vegetables like apricots, guava, watermelon, papaya, and pink grapefruit.

Buffalo Chicken Soup

Typical buffalo chicken dips, soups, and stews are made with a variety of cheeses and creamy ingredients. This deliciously spicy Paleo version incorporates creaminess without using any dairy products. The flavors in this warm, spicy soup make this meal very delightful on a cold fall day!

Serves 3–4

3 large chicken breasts
1½ cups Frank's Red Hot sauce, divided use
1 tablespoon clarified butter
1 tablespoon olive oil
1 large onion, roughly chopped
4 celery stalks, roughly chopped
1 large head cauliflower (grated, excluding stems)
1 tablespoon minced garlic
2 tablespoons lime juice
2 (28-ounce) containers chicken stock
1 cup unsweetened coconut milk
1 avocado, peeled, pitted, and sliced into thin pieces, for garnish
Cilantro, chopped, for garnish
Black pepper, to taste

1. Marinate the chicken breasts in 1 cup of Frank's Red Hot sauce in the refrigerator. Preheat the oven to 350°F. Place chicken and hot sauce marinade in a baking dish and bake for about 15 minutes, or until chicken breasts are cooked through fully. Remove from heat and shred into small, bite-size pieces.

2. In a large stock pot, melt clarified butter and olive oil over medium heat. Add chopped onion and celery and sauté for about 8–10 minutes. Add grated cauliflower and garlic and sauté for another 3 minutes. Add shredded chicken to pot and turn heat to medium-high. Add remaining ½ cup of hot sauce, lime juice, stock, and coconut milk. Bring to a boil. Turn heat down to low and simmer for about 10 minutes. Add more hot sauce to the broth now if you desire added heat.

3. Top with fresh avocado slices, cilantro, and black pepper to serve.

Curried Creamy Broccoli Soup

This hot Curried Creamy Broccoli Soup is an easy one-pot meal that incorporates many types of flavors! The bitterness of the broccoli blends with the sweet coconut milk and honey, and is topped off with the amazing spice from the curry and cayenne pepper. This soup can be enjoyed hot or cold, and is delicious when topped with a few large pieces of roasted broccoli!

Serves 3–4

2 tablespoons olive oil
1 large onion, chopped
2 cloves garlic, minced
½ tablespoon curry powder
½ teaspoon paprika
¼ teaspoon cayenne pepper
2½ pounds broccoli, chopped
3 cups vegetable broth
1 teaspoon raw organic honey
½ teaspoon salt
½ teaspoon pepper
1 cup coconut milk

1. Heat olive oil over medium heat in a large stock pot. Add chopped onion, garlic, curry powder, paprika, and cayenne pepper and sauté for about 6–7 minutes. Add broccoli, and turn heat up to medium-high. Add broth (only enough to cover all the vegetables), honey, salt, and pepper, and bring to a boil. Lower to a simmer for about 10 minutes, or until vegetables are tender.

2. Turn off heat and allow to cool slightly. Add coconut milk, and use an immersion blender to mix all ingredients to a smooth consistency. Once the desired consistency is reached, turn heat up to medium to heat through. Serve warm.

Spicy Avocado Soup

This smooth, green Spicy Avocado Soup is a creamy delight that can be sipped warmed or chilled. The green chilies in this recipe are what add the spice; they are an amazing, subtle ingredient used often in Mexican cuisine to help turn up the heat! The lime green color of the peppers blends nicely with the avocado in this recipe. *Note: Choose ripe avocados when making this Paleo dish to get the best taste and consistency.*

Serves 3–4

1 tablespoon olive oil
1 medium onion, chopped
1–2 jalapeños, seeded and chopped
1 tablespoon minced garlic
½ cup lime juice
1 canned green chili, chopped
1 (28-ounce) container vegetable broth
5 ripe avocados, pitted, peeled, and chopped

1. In a large stock pot, heat olive oil over medium-high heat. Add chopped onion and sauté for 5–6 minutes. Add chopped jalapeño and garlic and sauté for an additional 5–6 minutes. Add lime juice and green chili pepper and turn heat up to high. Stir ingredients.

2. Add broth and bring to a boil. Turn off heat to cool broth slightly. Add avocado chunks once cooled, and blend with an immersion blender until smooth.

3. Turn heat up to medium and simmer until warmed through (about 10 minutes). Serve warm.

🔥 MAKE A WELL-ROUNDED MEAL

Although this soup is healthy and nutrient-rich, it may not fill you up completely after a long day. To turn this into a one-pot meal, just add a little protein! Leftover shredded chicken, bacon bits, and tomato will turn this veggie soup into a hearty dinner dish.

Stuffed Pepper Soup

Stuffed peppers are a classic, homestyle dinner option, and this spiced-up, Paleo-friendly version really captures the rustic deliciousness of the real thing. This remake of the classic comfort food will warm you up inside and out, and if you're looking for even more warmth, add more serrano peppers for extra heat. This soup can be adjusted by using ground chicken or turkey as well!

Serves 4–6

1 tablespoon olive oil

1 large onion, chopped

2 large green peppers, chopped

2 serrano peppers, seeded and chopped

1 tablespoon minced garlic

2 heads cauliflower, grated (not including stems)

1 pound ground beef

1 teaspoon thyme

½ teaspoon cayenne pepper (add more for extra heat)

½ teaspoon salt and pepper

1 (28-ounce) can diced tomatoes, undrained

1 (28-ounce) container beef broth

Sliced avocado, for garnish

1. In a large stock pot, heat olive oil over medium-high heat. Add onion and sauté for about 8 minutes, stirring occasionally. Add green peppers and serrano peppers and sauté for an additional 5–6 minutes. Add garlic and cauliflower and continue to sauté for 3–4 more minutes.

2. Move vegetables aside in the stock pot. Cook beef in the center until browned and almost cooked through. Add thyme, cayenne pepper, salt, and pepper to the beef and stir. Add tomatoes and turn heat to high. Stir so tomatoes are well incorporated.

3. Add beef broth and bring to a boil. Simmer for about 10–15 minutes and serve with avocado slices.

Curried Cauliflower Soup

This six-ingredient concoction is simple, but the flavor is anything but! The curry, cumin, and coriander spice up this dish and provide a fragrant Middle Eastern flavor. And if you want to make the soup look as hot as it tastes, consider using orange cauliflower instead of white cauliflower. Orange cauliflower has 25 percent more vitamin A than white cauliflower and lends an attractive color to the soup. For additional flavor, add a large onion or shallots to this recipe.

1. Place all the ingredients into a 4-quart slow cooker. Stir. Cook on low for 8 hours.

2. Use an immersion blender, or blend the soup in batches in a standard blender, until smooth.

Serves 4

1 pound cauliflower florets
2½ cups water
1 medium onion, minced
2 cloves garlic, minced
3 teaspoons curry powder
¼ teaspoon cumin
¼ teaspoon coriander

🌶 CURRY POWDER POWER

Curry powder is a mixture of spices commonly used in South Asian cooking. While it does not correlate directly to any particular kind of curry, it is popular in Europe and North America to add an Indian flair to dishes. Curry powder can contain any number of spices, but nearly always includes turmeric, which gives it its distinctive yellow color.

Southwestern Soup

A zesty and hearty creation that encompasses the perfect balance of herbs and seasonings, this Southwestern Soup is sure to bring the heat to your table. The impact of the spicy veggies like jalapeño and green pepper, blended amongst the heat from cumin and chili powder, produce a powerful potpourri of fragrance, flair, and fiery flavor! Experiment with additional veggies like red pepper and carrots, or add beef tenderloin in place of pork to make this a slightly richer dish.

Serves 4

1 pound pork tenderloin, cut into 1" pieces
1 cup chopped onion
1 green bell pepper, seeded and chopped
1 jalapeño, seeded and minced
2 cloves garlic, minced
1 teaspoon chili powder
1 teaspoon ground cumin
¼ teaspoon freshly ground black pepper
5 cups chicken stock
1 (14-ounce) can diced tomatoes
1 cup diced fresh avocado, for garnish
2 tablespoons chopped fresh cilantro leaves, for garnish
Lime wedges, for garnish

1. In the bottom of a 6-quart slow cooker, combine the pork, onion, bell pepper, jalapeño, garlic, chili powder, cumin, and black pepper and stir to combine. Add stock and tomatoes. Cover and cook on low for 6–8 hours or on high for 3–4 hours.

2. When ready to serve, ladle soup into bowls and top with avocado and cilantro. Garnish soup with lime wedges.

Chicken Chili Verde

This spicy chili will be a big hit at your next Cinco de Mayo party! Enjoy this thick and chunky chili over a Southwestern-themed vegetable medley or cauliflower rice, or eliminate the water and juice from the canned vegetables to make the filling for Mexican-style lettuce wraps! This is also a great recipe for leftover roasted chicken. Just shred and add in place of the cubes of chicken. Avocado slices serve well as a festive garnish. But however you choose to serve this Chicken Chili Verde, be sure to have something on hand to soothe your fiery tongue!

Heat the oil in a skillet over medium heat. Add the chicken and cook, stirring frequently, until the chicken is browned on all sides; about 1–2 minutes per side. Place browned chicken in a greased 4–6-quart slow cooker, then add the remaining ingredients. Cover and cook on high for 3 hours or on low for 6 hours.

Serves 8

½ tablespoon olive oil

2 pounds skinless, boneless chicken breast, cubed

2 (28-ounce) cans whole peeled tomatoes, undrained

1 (4-ounce) can diced green chili peppers, undrained

1 teaspoon thyme

1 teaspoon oregano

1 teaspoon basil

1 tablespoon chili powder

2 teaspoons cumin

1 tablespoon raw organic honey

1 large onion, minced

3 cloves garlic, minced

½ cup water

Texas Firehouse Chili

This no-bean chili is similar to dishes entered into firehouse chili cook-offs all over Texas. This hot, Southwestern-style chili is full of spice, and the best part of the dish is how the smokiness from the chipotle pepper melds with the fire-roasted diced tomatoes, creating a filling, mouthwatering meal. By cooking this Texas Firehouse Chili slowly in the slow cooker, the cubed beef is broken down into small, melt-in-your-mouth pieces of flavorful protein. Enjoy hot with chopped green onions and sliced avocados on top!

Serves 4

1 pound cubed lean beef
2 tablespoons onion powder
1 tablespoon garlic powder
2 tablespoons Mexican-style
  chili powder
1 tablespoon paprika
½ teaspoon oregano
½ teaspoon freshly ground
  black pepper
½ teaspoon white pepper
½ teaspoon cayenne pepper
½ teaspoon chipotle pepper
1 (14-ounce) can tomato purée
1 (14-ounce) can fire-roasted
  diced tomatoes

1. Quickly brown the beef for 5–7 minutes in a nonstick skillet. Drain off any excess grease.

2. Add the meat and all of the remaining ingredients to a 4-quart slow cooker. Cook on low for up to 10 hours.

Picante Pumpkin Chicken Chili

If you're looking for a sweet and spicy dish, sit down and enjoy this warming, fall-flavored chili. There are so many layers of flavor in the chili, and the longer you let it simmer, the more pronounced this layered heat will be! Feel free to add more cayenne pepper or additional chilies to accentuate the savory flavors.

1. In a large Dutch oven, heat olive oil over medium heat. Add onion and sauté for about 6 minutes, or until translucent. Add peppers, chilis, and garlic, and sauté for another 6–7 minutes.

2. Add pumpkin, tomatoes, and all spices. Bring to a boil, stirring occasionally. Turn heat to low. Let chili simmer on low for about 30 minutes, or until flavors start to meld together. The longer, the better!

3. Add shredded chicken and stir for an additional 10 minutes. Serve warm with chopped cilantro and a few slices of avocado on top.

Serves 6

2 tablespoons olive oil
1 large yellow onion, chopped
2 large red bell peppers, chopped
2 large canned green chilis, chopped
2 tablespoons minced garlic
1 (14-ounce) can pumpkin purée
1 (14-ounce) can diced tomatoes (not drained)
1 (14-ounce) can ground peeled tomatoes
1 tablespoon chili powder
1 tablespoon ground cumin
1 tablespoon paprika
1 teaspoon cinnamon
1 teaspoon nutmeg
1 teaspoon each salt and pepper
½ teaspoon cayenne pepper (or more for added spice)
1 pound chicken breasts, cooked and shredded
Chopped cilantro, for garnish
1–2 avocados, pitted and sliced, for garnish

Hot and Spicy Summer Squash Soup

This delicious curried soup is perfect in the summer months when squash is plentiful and ripe and you don't want to spend hours in the kitchen. And, if you find yourself craving it in the wintertime, know that it can be enjoyed chilled or warm. The compilation of garlic, curry powder, ginger, and paprika create an absolutely astounding flavor and aroma, so kick back and enjoy this Hot and Spicy Summer Squash Soup with a light salad or a piece of grilled chicken.

Serves 3–4

1 tablespoon olive oil
½ yellow onion, roughly chopped
½ teaspoon minced garlic
2 large summer squash, roughly chopped
1 (28-ounce) container vegetable stock
1 teaspoon curry powder
1 teaspoon ground ginger
¼ teaspoon paprika
1 teaspoon each salt and pepper
½ cup chopped green onion

1. In a medium sauce pot, heat olive oil over medium heat. Add onion and cook for about 5–6 minutes. (Make sure onion is translucent and does not brown.) Add garlic and summer squash and sauté for about 8–10 minutes, until squash is soft.

2. Add the remaining ingredients (except for the chopped green onion) and bring to a boil. Turn heat to low and let simmer for about 10 minutes. Remove from heat.

3. Once cooled slightly, blend mixture (in food processor or with immersion blender) until smooth. Serve warm or chilled, topped with chopped green onions.

🔥 SQUASH SWAP

Various types of squash can be enjoyed in this recipe. Butternut and acorn squash will turn this soup into a sweeter, smoother meal. These types of squash are called "winter squash," as they are most prevalent in the fall and winter months in the United States. If you're using butternut or acorn squash in this recipe, a teaspoon of nutmeg is another delicious addition to the ingredients list.

Wintery Italian Wedding Soup

This traditional soup is made with rice or pasta, but is just as warming and delicious without it in this Paleo-friendly version. This soup is super easy to make. Try adding a little extra spice to this recipe with more red pepper flakes, a dash of hot sauce, and perhaps some chunks of roasted red pepper. It makes it the perfect concoction for a cold winter's day!

1. Add olive oil to a large stock pot over medium-high heat. Add bison meatballs and pan fry until they are browned (about 4–5 minutes). Add minced garlic and escarole and sauté for a minute more. Add beef broth and spices and bring to a boil. Turn heat to medium and cook until escarole leaves start to wilt, about 7–8 minutes.

2. Whisk the eggs in a mixing bowl. Start to stir soup in a circular motion in the stock pot. Gradually pour in scrambled eggs, so they wisp into the broth. Serve immediately with fresh basil garnish.

Serves 4

2 tablespoons olive oil
20 bison meatballs, raw (see Bison Meatballs and Fiery Marinara recipe in Chapter 2)
1 teaspoon minced garlic
1 head escarole lettuce
2 (28-ounce) containers beef broth (replace with chicken broth for a lighter taste)
½ teaspoon dried basil
½ teaspoon dried oregano
½ teaspoon red pepper flakes
2 eggs, scrambled
Fresh basil, chopped, for garnish

🔥 MEATY MADNESS

Bison meatballs are not the only type of protein that can be used in this recipe. In fact, beef meatballs are the traditional ingredients, but it's fun to be creative when trying this at home! If you want to mix it up, hot chorizo sausage patties make a great (spicier) replacement. Also, veal, chicken, or turkey meatballs work just as well. You can also try combining different types of meat for the meatballs (like beef and veal) for another tasty option.

Vegetarian Chili

This is the ultimate way to eat a spicy, satisfying Paleo chili with no guilt! This thick concoction is packed with hearty vegetables, spicy peppers, and a ton of fiery flavor. There are many different ways to enjoy this Vegetarian Chili—in a bowl with avocado, accompanying eggs for breakfast, or on top of a hamburger!

Serves 4

2 tablespoons olive oil

1 large onion, roughly chopped

3 bell peppers, chopped (orange, red, and yellow, for color)

3 large portobello mushroom caps, finely chopped

1 pound (about 1½ cups) butternut squash, peeled, seeded, and chopped

2 large chipotle peppers in adobo, chopped

2 jalapeños, seeded and chopped

1 tablespoon minced garlic

Juice of ½ lime

1 tablespoon ground cumin

1–2 tablespoons chili powder

1 tablespoon paprika

½ teaspoon cayenne pepper

Salt and pepper, to taste

1 (28-ounce) can diced tomatoes

1 (28-ounce) can ground peeled tomatoes

1 tablespoon tomato paste

Chopped cilantro, for garnish

1–2 avocados, pitted and sliced, for garnish

1. Heat olive oil in a Dutch oven over medium high heat. Sauté the onion, bell peppers, mushrooms, and butternut squash for 6–7 minutes, or until they are soft. Add chipotle peppers, jalapeños, garlic, lime juice, and all spices and sauté for an additional 3–4 minutes.

2. Turn heat to high, and add all tomatoes and tomato paste to the pot. Once boiling, turn heat to medium-low and simmer for 30 minutes (at least). Top with chopped cilantro and sliced avocado.

Coconut Curry Soup with Shrimp

Southeast Asian dishes are known for how beautifully they balance flavor, and this Thai-inspired dish balances sweet shrimp with creamy coconut and spicy curry. This tasty dish is sure to open your airways with its authentic heat and creamy finish. For more spice, add extra red curry paste, but be cautious; a little goes a long way.

1. Heat clarified butter over medium-high heat in a medium stock pot. Sprinkle salt and pepper on shrimp and sauté on both sides for 1–2 minutes. Remove from pot and place on a separate dish.

2. Add all other ingredients (except for the chives) to the stock pot and stir. Turn up the heat and bring to a boil. Whisk ingredients together and add shrimp back into the pot. Heat for another 5 minutes and serve with chives.

Serves 2–3

1 teaspoon clarified butter
Salt and pepper, to taste
6 large raw shrimp, shelled and deveined
1 teaspoon sesame oil
1 teaspoon red curry paste
2 cups chicken broth
1 cup coconut milk
1 tablespoon grated ginger
¼ teaspoon garlic paste
Pinch cayenne pepper
Juice of 1 lime
Chives cut into thin strands, for garnish

Kickin' Kimchi Soup

Kimchi is a fermented Korean dish that has a very pungent odor and spicy taste. While normal Kimchi should be fermented for more than 72 hours, this soup can be whipped up in a short amount of time. It still manages to showcase the same flavors and hotness thanks to the cayenne pepper and hot chili powder!

Serves 3–4

1 tablespoon olive oil
1 head cabbage, sliced into thin pieces.
3 cups chicken broth
1 tablespoon minced garlic
1 tablespoon grated ginger
1 teaspoon raw organic honey
1 teaspoon hot chili powder
1 teaspoon cayenne pepper (or more for added spice)
Salt and pepper, to taste
Sliced green onions, for garnish

1. In a large stock pot, heat olive oil over medium-high heat. Add cabbage and sauté for about 3 minutes, until it starts to brown slightly.

2. Add all other ingredients and bring to a boil. Boil gently for about 15 minutes, stirring often. Serve when cabbage is soft and the desired spiciness is reached.

🔥 KIMCHI IN KOREAN CULTURE

Kimchi is a native dish of Korea, and is used to create a wide range of dishes like soups, stews, and rice. It is a form of pickled vegetables and has ancient roots within the Korean culture. Hot chili powder is the star ingredient in this spicy jarred treat. The most commonly used version of kimchi is red in color; however, white kimchi—a non-spicy version—does not exhibit a red hue.

Spiced Carrot Ginger Soup

The carrots and ginger used in this hot and spicy recipe make for a beautiful flavor combination. When these two sweet ingredients are added to savory ingredients like onions and garlic, they create a smooth concoction that will just melt in your mouth! The paprika and cloves add a bit of heat to this recipe, while the coconut milk brings in a subtle creaminess. This delectable soup is great any time of year and can be eaten warm or chilled.

1. Cook coconut oil, garlic, and onion in a saucepan over medium heat until the onions are soft. Then add the carrots, broth, coconut milk, ginger, paprika, cloves, and a pinch of salt and pepper. Cook for about 15 minutes, until the carrots are soft.

2. Place all ingredients in a food processor or blender and mix until smooth and creamy. Top with more ginger, if desired, and serve!

Serves 3–4

2 tablespoons coconut oil
3 cloves garlic, minced
½ yellow onion, finely chopped
3 cups chopped carrots
2 cups vegetable broth
1 (14-ounce) can coconut milk
3–4 tablespoons fresh ginger, minced
1 tablespoon paprika
1 tablespoon cloves
Salt and pepper, to taste

CHAPTER 4

Entrées

Main entrées specific to the Paleolithic diet can range from super-simple to intricately complex. Fortunately, the flavor, aroma, and seasoning exhibit just as much versatility and flexibility as the dishes themselves. In this chapter you'll find a number of common recipes that have traditionally involved throwing a piece of meat in the oven or slow cooker—ranging from Pepper-Crusted Steak to Racy Rub Roast to Grilled Jerk Pork Loin—and some adaptions and reinventions of some non-Paleo "comfort food" staples like Zesty Paleo Meatloaf, Chipotle Chicken Casserole, and Beef and Squash Pot Pie. Each of these recipes have been delightfully intensified with the use of a spectrum of fiery, zesty, and fragrant herbs, spices, veggies, and more. Fresh herbs and spices like cayenne pepper, cilantro, red pepper flakes, garlic, and ginger are used to create hot, spicy, and delicious Paleo-friendly entrées, sure to satisfy even the most daring palate. Many of the recipes included here offer some unique flavors that standard American fare doesn't regularly encompass. For example, coconut butter, oil, and milk; hot chilies; Sriracha; and habanero peppers are a few of the key ingredients used to produce numerous jaw-dropping and irresistible main dishes. Enjoy!

Coconut Chicken Tenders with a Kick

Moist yet crispy, perfectly spicy thanks to red pepper and cayenne, yet gloriously sweet at the same time, these Coconut Chicken Tenders with a Kick are absolute perfection! If you want to mix things up a bit, the Mango Salsa from the Spiced Salmon with Salsa recipe in this chapter is an excellent substitute for the homemade honey mustard used here.

Serves 2–3

2 chicken breasts
2 tablespoons coconut flour
¼ teaspoon sea salt
¼ teaspoon white pepper
¼ teaspoon crushed red pepper flakes
Pinch cayenne pepper
1 egg
1 cup unsweetened shredded coconut
2 tablespoons coconut oil
2 tablespoons Dijon mustard
1 tablespoon raw organic honey

1. Slice chicken breasts lengthwise into tenders (approximately 4 per breast), then place three bowls on counter (for the "breading" process). Fill the first bowl with coconut flour, salt, pepper, red pepper flakes, and cayenne pepper. Fill the second bowl with 1 egg (scramble in the bowl). Fill third bowl with unsweetened coconut. Take each tender and dredge with the flour mixture, dip in egg, and coat with coconut. Place coated chicken on a plate.

2. Heat coconut oil in large skillet over medium heat. Add chicken tenders in batches, and cook approximately 5 minutes per side, or until chicken is cooked through and coconut flakes are golden brown.

3. Whisk Dijon mustard and honey together in small bowl. Serve as a dip with chicken tenders.

♨ ALMOND FLOUR

Almond flour (or almond meal) is made from finely ground blanched almonds. Almond flour is gluten-free, and can be used as a substitute for white or wheat flour in a variety of non-Paleo recipes. Improve its shelf life by storing it in an airtight container in the fridge or freezer.

Racy Maki Rolls

The jalapeños and red pepper used in this recipe really heat these simple traditional sushi rolls to a fiery degree of *hot*. Also, the addition of the Fiery Fried "Rice" from Chapter 5 creates the need for a "Use Caution" sign before delving into these Paleo-friendly maki. If you want to be super daring, add a dollop of wasabi to each slice before dipping in the coconut aminos.

1. Gently combine the carrots, cucumber, avocado, and jalapeños in a bowl. Place 1 seaweed sheet on top of a sushi rolling mat or similar surface. Using a rice paddle or spatula, place ½ cup rice on the seaweed evenly over half of the sheet. Place about 1 ounce salmon and about ⅛ of the vegetable fillings from the bowl on top of the cauliflower.

2. When you've finished adding your fillings, use the end of your sushi mat to roll up the sheet with everything inside. Toward the end of the sheet of seaweed, lightly brush the end of the sheet with lime juice. This will help seal the roll.

3. Finish rolling and press to ensure the roll is tight. Slice the roll into 6–8 pieces. Sprinkle the top of the roll with a pinch of red pepper flakes. Repeat for the remaining sheets of seaweed, until all of the salmon, cauliflower, and vegetable filling is used up. Serve the Maki Rolls with coconut aminos for dipping.

Yields 8 rolls

1 medium carrot, peeled and thinly sliced, for filling

½ medium cucumber, peeled thinly sliced, for filling

1 avocado, sliced into small pieces, for filling

2–4 jalapeños, finely chopped, for filling

8 sheets roasted seaweed

4 cups Fiery Fried "Rice," for filling (see Chapter 5)

8–10 ounces sashimi-grade salmon, sliced into strips the same length as the sheets of seaweed

1 tablespoon lime juice

2–3 tablespoons crushed red pepper flakes, for garnish

Coconut aminos, for dipping

🔥 SOY SAUCE SUBSTITUTE

Coconut aminos are one Paleo-approved substitute for soy sauce, often used for dipping sushi. You can also use a combination of canola or olive oil, with some lemon or lime juice as well. Add a sprinkling of fresh herbs and spices for a subtle hint of seasoning and a pinch of zest.

Paleolithic TurChiDuc

A recipe sure to add a serious *wow* factor to your next holiday feast, this protein-packed, super-spiced poultry dish is a guaranteed crowd pleaser. It's sure to leave some eyes watering, and mouths watering for more! There is a lot of room for flexibility here, so feel free to use almonds and walnuts in addition to the pecans in the stuffing, and if you're feeling really adventurous, try using some additions from the pepper family too.

Serves 12–14

5 cups Seasonably Seasoned Stuffing (see Chapter 5)
½ cup Spicy Cranberry Chutney (see Chapter 5)
¼ cup chopped pecans
4 tablespoons coconut butter
2 tablespoons fresh thyme leaves
6 fresh sage leaves
2 tablespoons red pepper flakes
3 cloves garlic, cut in quarters
1 (10- to 12-pound) turkey, deboned
1 tablespoon olive oil
Sea salt and freshly ground black pepper, to taste
½ teaspoon cayenne pepper
1 (4- to 5-pound) duck, deboned
1 (3- to 4-pound) chicken, deboned

1. Preheat the oven to 300°F.

2. Measure out 2¼ cups of stuffing and set aside. Place 1 cup of stuffing in another bowl along with the Spicy Cranberry Chutney and pecans. Toss gently to combine. In a third bowl, place remaining 1¾ cups stuffing aside. You should have 3 separate bowls of stuffing.

3. In a blender or food processor fitted with the metal blade, combine coconut butter, thyme, sage, red pepper flakes, and garlic until herbs are finely chopped.

4. Run your hand under the skin of the turkey to separate and make a pocket, but do not separate the skin completely from the meat. Distribute the butter-herb mixture evenly under the skin. Then rub the skin of the turkey with the olive oil. Sprinkle generously with sea salt and freshly ground pepper.

5. Flip the turkey over so it is open and skin-side down. Sprinkle with salt, black pepper, and cayenne pepper, then spread the first bowl of stuffing evenly over the turkey cavity. Place the duck on top of the stuffing, skin-side down. Spread the cranberry-nut stuffing on top of the open duck cavity. Top with the chicken, skin-side down. Spread the third bowl of stuffing on top of the open chicken cavity.

6. Skewer the back of the chicken closed. Bring up the sides of the duck to cover the chicken. Skewer the back of the duck closed. Repeat the process with the turkey. Carefully turn the TurChiDuc over, so it is seam-side down and breast-side up. Remove all skewers except the last one holding the turkey together.

7. Place the TurChiDuc in a heavy roaster pan. Roast 3½–4½ hours, until a meat thermometer inserted in the center of the chicken stuffing reaches 165°F. Baste once per hour with pan juices. Let TurChiDuc sit for about 30–40 minutes before carving. To serve, slice the TurChiDuc across the breast to show off each layer.

🔥 AVOID FOOD-BORNE ILLNESS

Be sure to refrigerate all of the deboned birds until ready for use. Do not add the stuffing and assemble the TurChiDuc until you are ready to cook it to prevent the stuffing from becoming contaminated. Consider removing the wings completely from the duck and the chicken to make carving easier.

Fire-Grilled Fish Tacos

This fiery twist on fish is a versatile dish, which means there are a variety of ways to kick up this recipe. Red and green peppers, hot sauce, and salsa are called for in the recipe, but don't stop there! Try this dish with jalapeños, habanero peppers, Sriracha sauce, or whatever other spicy ingredients you desire.

Serves 4

2 cups chopped white onion
¾ cup chopped fresh cilantro
¼ cup olive oil
3 tablespoons lime juice
3 tablespoons freshly squeezed orange juice
2 tablespoons hot sauce
2 cloves garlic, minced
1 teaspoon dried oregano
1 pound tilapia, or other fish of your choice
1 teaspoon sea salt and black pepper
4 Cauliflower or Coconut Flour Tortillas (see recipes for the Spicy Chicken Tacos with Cauliflower Tortillas and Spicy Beef Tacos with Coconut Flour Tortillas in this chapter)
2 avocados, peeled and sliced
1 red and 1 green bell pepper, thinly sliced
½ small head cabbage, thinly sliced
Slow-Cooked Spicy Salsa (see Chapter 6), or jarred
Lime wedges, for garnish

1. Stir 1 cup onion, ¼ cup cilantro, oil, lime juice, orange juice, hot sauce, garlic, and oregano in medium bowl. Sprinkle fish with sea salt and pepper. Spread half of the onion mixture over the bottom of a 9" × 13" glass baking dish.

2. Arrange fish atop onion mixture. Spoon remaining onion mixture over fish. Cover and chill for about 1 hour, flipping halfway through.

3. Grill fish on medium-high heat until just opaque in the center, 3–5 minutes per side. Lightly char the (coconut or cauliflower) tortillas.

4. Chop the cooked fish, and place on a serving platter with tortillas, remaining 1 cup chopped onion, remaining ½ cup cilantro, avocados, red and green peppers, cabbage, salsa, and lime wedges.

Blazing Meatballs and Sizzling Summer Veggies

With the combination of jalapeño peppers and cayenne pepper embedded in the meat, and the fiery coating from the Chipotle Tomato Sauce, these Blazing Meatballs and Sizzling Summer Veggies are nothing short of scorching! Try using plain marinara if a more toned-down version is preferred. For an even hotter end result, add a few sliced jalapeños and/or habanero peppers to the veggie mix.

1. In a large bowl, combine ground beef, minced garlic, jalapeños, 1 teaspoon sea salt, and cayenne pepper. Create 30–35 evenly formed meatballs and set them on a plate.

2. In a large nonstick skillet, heat coconut butter and 1 tablespoon oil over high heat. Add meatballs in a single layer and cook until deep brown on all sides. Sprinkle the tops with garlic powder, oregano, and a pinch more sea salt. Drain the excess fat. Add the Chipotle Tomato Sauce and stir until all meatballs are evenly coated. Add ⅛ cup of fresh basil and bring to a boil. Lower heat, cover, and simmer about 15 minutes or until meatballs are tender and done.

3. While meatballs are simmering, prepare the vegetables. Coat the vegtables in 1 tablespoon canola oil, and sprinkle evenly with 1 teaspoon sea salt. Grill over medium-high heat until lightly charred and soft. Remove from heat and slice into smaller pieces.

4. Place cooked vegetables in serving bowls, top with meatballs and sauce, and garnish with the remaining fresh basil.

Yields 30–35 meatballs (Serves 4–6)

2 pounds lean ground beef
2 tablespoons garlic, minced
3 jalapeños, finely chopped
2 teaspoons sea salt
½ teaspoon cayenne pepper
1 tablespoon coconut butter
2 tablespoons canola oil
½ teaspoon garlic powder
½ teaspoon oregano
24 ounces Chipotle Tomato Sauce (see Chapter 2)
¼ cup fresh basil, thinly sliced
6 large tomatoes, cut in half
2 red bell peppers, cut in half and seeded
2 zucchini, cut into ¼"-long slices

Spiced Sweet Potato Latkes

Latkes are a traditional Hanukkah dish, and this recipe adds a very pleasing sweet and spicy twist. Nutmeg is used in this recipe, but it can be substituted with cloves if desired. A dash of fiery hot sauce like Sriracha would kick up the spice even more. Cardamom is another addition that would add a bit more pep to these potatoes.

Yields 8 latkes

2 sweet potatoes, peeled and shredded
2 eggs, lightly beaten
1 tablespoon raw organic honey
2 tablespoons almond flour
1 teaspoon ground nutmeg
2 teaspoons ground ginger
2 teaspoons ground cinnamon
1 teaspoon paprika
¼ cup canola oil

1. Place sweet potatoes in a colander. Place some cheesecloth over the potatoes, and squeeze the potatoes to release as much liquid as possible. Let the potatoes sit to release more liquid, then squeeze again.

2. In a large bowl, combine sweet potatoes, eggs, honey, almond flour, nutmeg, ginger, cinnamon, and paprika. Mix well.

3. Heat oil in large heavy skillet to 375°F. Form the above mixture into pancake-size latkes, and fry in the hot oil. Flip the latkes after 2–3 minutes (when bottom is browned) and brown other side. Drain on paper towels, and serve piping hot!

🔥 SWEET POTATOES HIGHLY ENCOURAGED IN PRIMAL FARE

Typically classified as a Paleo "No" food item, sweet potatoes are super nutritious and therefore strongly recommended as an important variation to the Paleo diet. Sweet potatoes are jam-packed with vitamins A and C, potassium, and fiber. They help restore depleted glycogen levels after intense cardiovascular activity, which can be quite challenging for strict Paleo followers without the incorporation of some nutrient-dense carbohydrates.

Peppery Pork Roast

This Peppery Pork Roast cooks in almost no time, making it a quick and delicious weeknight dinner. Simple seasonings like chili powder, paprika, cumin, ginger, thyme, and black pepper add a bit of a bite and a whole lot of flavor to this pork without overpowering it! Enjoy this hearty meat alongside a medley of root veggies and a fresh green salad.

1. In a small bowl, mix together chili powder, paprika, cumin, ginger, thyme, and black pepper. Rub spice mix onto the pork. Place meat in a baking dish, cover, and refrigerate for 2–3 hours.

2. Preheat the grill to medium heat. Cook for 30 minutes, or to desired tenderness, turning to cook evenly.

Serves 6

2 tablespoons chili powder
2 tablespoons paprika
1 tablespoon ground cumin
1 teaspoon ground ginger
1½ teaspoons dried thyme
1 teaspoon black pepper
2 pounds pork tenderloin (2 [1-pound] roasts)

Spiced Cider–Soaked Roast of Turkey

This incredibly moist and flavorful Spiced Cider–Soaked Roast of Turkey is the most amazing-tasting turkey ever! Soaking the turkey in a saltwater and cider brine produces tender, juicy, melt-in-your mouth meat. The savory seasonings, including the black and red pepper, thyme, paprika, and cayenne provide the perfect amount of pep to this bird. Keep in mind that a brined turkey cooks 20–30 minutes faster, so be sure to watch your clock. Enjoy!

Serves 10–12

1 cup sea salt
1 cup raw organic honey
1 tablespoon black pepper
1 tablespoon dried thyme
8 cloves garlic, crushed
12 cups apple cider
1 (12- to 14-pound) whole turkey, neck and giblets removed
1 tablespoon paprika
1 tablespoon garlic powder
1½ teaspoons crushed red pepper
1½ teaspoons onion powder
1½ tablespoons dried leaf oregano
1 teaspoon cayenne pepper
¼ cup melted coconut butter

1. Combine salt, honey, black pepper, thyme, and garlic with 6 cups of the apple cider in a stock pot over medium-high heat; bring to a boil. Reduce heat, and simmer 10 minutes or until honey and salt have fully dissolved. Stir in remaining 6 cups apple cider. Cool mixture completely.

2. Rinse turkey with cold water. Place in a (leak-free) turkey-size oven bag, add the cider mixture, and tightly secure the bag. Refrigerate 12–24 hours, turning periodically.

3. Remove turkey from the bag and discard brine. Rinse turkey with cold water, drain, and pat dry with paper towels. Combine all the remaining spices together in a bowl.

4. Loosen the skin from the turkey, without totally detaching skin; spread 1 tablespoon of the seasoning mixture under skin, and sprinkle 1 tablespoon inside turkey cavity. Sprinkle turkey skin with remaining seasoning.

5. Preheat the oven to 325°F. Place the turkey breast-side up on a roasting rack, and brush with the melted coconut butter. Roast about 3 hours, or until the internal temperature reaches 180°F. Brush with pan juices periodically during the last hour of cooking. Remove from heat and allow turkey to rest for 15–20 minutes before carving.

St. Patrick's Smoked Shoulder

This Gaelic-inspired dish packs a serious kick of spice, so get into the spirit of St. Patrick's Day all year round and create a little Irish luck of your own at your next family gathering! Ironically, corned beef isn't distinctly Irish, as it is more of an Irish-American tradition and often enjoyed alongside a tall glass of stout. This spiced-up version is even more nontraditional with the incorporation of cayenne pepper, cloves, cinnamon, and an absolutely to-die-for chili sauce glaze. This will make even the bravest of leprechauns beg for more Guinness to douse the flames from this spicy fire!

1. In a large stock pot, combine all of the ingredients (except for the chili sauce, 1 cup water, and honey) and cover with warm water. Bring to a boil and simmer, covered, over medium-low heat for 40 minutes per pound, approximately 2½ hours, until the meat is tender. Remove the beef from the stock pot; cover, cool, and refrigerate overnight.

2. Slice the meat very thin and place slices in a baking dish. Preheat the oven to 350°F.

3. Make the glaze by combining the chili sauce and water, and pour just enough glaze over the beef to moisten it well. Drizzle the honey over the top and bake uncovered for 30 minutes, or until the meat is heated through.

Serves 4–6

- 5–6 pound cut of corned beef
- ¼ teaspoon dried rosemary
- 1 bay leaf
- 1 teaspoon dill seed
- 1 teaspoon cayenne pepper
- 6 whole cloves
- 1 cinnamon stick
- 1 clove garlic
- 1 yellow onion, cut into small cubes
- 2 large celery sticks, cut into small cubes
- ½ orange, unpeeled, cut into small cubes
- ½ cup chili sauce
- 1 cup water
- ⅓ cup raw organic honey

🔥 NOT YOUR AVERAGE IRISH DINNER

Corned beef is traditionally slow cooked or boiled simultaneously with Irish staples like cabbage, carrots, and potatoes. So why aren't these vegetables in the pot with the corned beef? For one reason, vegetables shouldn't cook that long. And secondly, vegetables cooked with the meat always end up looking discolored and lifeless. Cooking them separately allows the vegetables to maintain their color, nutrients, and most importantly, their flavor.

Prosciutto-Hugged Holiday Chicken

Hot peppers and red pepper flakes really heat up this richly flavored, succulent holiday dish. The prosciutto creates the perfect degree of saltiness while helping to contain and preserve the magnificent flavor through each and every memorable bite. Pork tenderloin also works well in this recipe, and you can increase the amount of jalapeños and/or red pepper flakes if you really want to fire up your guests!

Serves 4

3 tablespoons canola oil
Salt and pepper, to taste
1 small onion, peeled and quartered
1 red bell pepper, sliced
1 jalapeño, sliced
2–3 tomatillos, halved
2 tablespoons rosemary
2 tablespoons sage
2 cloves garlic, minced
1 tablespoon red pepper flakes
4 (6–8-ounce) boneless chicken breasts, pounded thin
4–8 thin slices of prosciutto (1–2 slices per chicken breast)

1. Preheat the oven to 400°F. In a food processor or blender, add the canola oil, salt, pepper, onion, bell pepper, jalapeño, tomatillos, rosemary, sage, garlic, and red pepper flakes and blend until smooth.

2. Coat both sides of the chicken breasts with half of the mixture. Place a chicken breast on top of 1–2 slices of prosciutto, and starting at one end, tightly roll the prosciutto and chicken together to form a roll. Secure with a toothpick. Repeat for remaining chicken breasts.

3. Add more of the spicy oil mixture to each roll of chicken and prosciutto, saving the second half of the sauce in a separate container for use before serving. Remove toothpicks and place rolls seam-side down onto a foil-lined baking sheet.

4. Bake for 30–40 minutes. Remove from heat and allow to sit for 5–10 minutes. Slice the rolls and drizzle the remaining oil mixture over the finished product. Serve immediately.

Sweet Potato and Kale Quesadillas with Coconut Flour Tortillas

This combination of flavors is absolute perfection! This Paleo quesadilla recipe produces a dish that encompasses so many delectable flavors—sweet, spicy, savory—all of which are really revved-up with the fiery combination of cumin, chili powder, and some chipotle peppers in adobo sauce. This recipe right here more than just pleases the palate, it is lip-smacking g-o-o-d!

1. Add the potatoes to a large saucepan and add enough water until the potatoes are about covered, and bring water to a boil (over high heat). Reduce heat to medium and simmer for about 15 minutes, until the potatoes are tender. Drain, then pour into a large bowl. Mash the potatoes and add the salt, cumin, chili powder, oregano, and chipotle peppers. Mix until well combined.

2. In a medium skillet, heat the olive oil over medium heat. Add in the kale and green onions. Cook until the kale is bright green and tender. Add the kale and onion mixture to the mashed sweet potatoes. Add in the tomatoes and mix until combined.

3. Using a spatula, spread about ⅓–½ cup of the filling on half of a tortilla. Fold the empty half of the tortilla. Repeat with the remaining tortillas.

4. Cook the quesadillas in a skillet over medium-high heat until browned, flipping half-way through. Serve with fresh vegetables and a hot sauce/salsa of your choice.

Serves 4–6

3 medium sweet potatoes, cut into ½"-thick slices
¼ teaspoon salt, divided use
½ teaspoon cumin
½ teaspoon chili powder
¼ teaspoon oregano
1–2 chipotle peppers in adobo, minced
½ tablespoon olive oil
3 cups chopped kale
3 green onions, thinly sliced
1–2 cups tomatoes, diced
8–10 large coconut flour tortillas (see Spicy Beef Tacos recipe in this chapter)

Vivacious Veggie Layer Lasagna

A fired-up, caveman-approved vegetarian recipe that will instantly heat up your taste buds, this zesty dish is packed full of fiber, nutrients, anti-oxidants, and absolutely fantastic flavor! This veggie lasagna can also be made using the Chipotle Tomato Sauce or Jalapeño Tomatillo Sauce, both found in Chapter 2. Enjoy this vivacious creation after a warm bowl of Tasty Tomato or Spicy Avocado Soup, both found in Chapter 3, for a super-healthy, meat-free, hot and spicy, complete meal.

Serves 4–6

For Lasagna:

2 large zucchini, sliced lengthwise into ¼"–½" thick slices

1 eggplant, sliced lengthwise into ½" slices

1 red bell pepper, quartered and seeded

10–12 trimmed asparagus spears, chopped

2 tablespoons canola oil

½ teaspoon cumin

½ teaspoon red pepper flakes

½ teaspoon sea salt

½ teaspoon black pepper

1 tablespoon rosemary

10 thyme sprigs

½ cup chopped fresh basil leaves

For Sauce:

1 thinly sliced onion

2 cloves garlic, minced

1 tablespoon olive oil

½ teaspoon red pepper flakes

½ tablespoon dried oregano

1 tablespoon tomato paste

1 (14-ounce) can plum tomatoes

1. **For Lasagna:** Brush vegetables with canola oil and sprinkle with cumin, red pepper flakes, sea salt, pepper, rosemary, and thyme sprigs. Roast the slices of zucchini, eggplant, and bell pepper at 400°F for 20–25 minutes, or until soft.

2. Remove the zucchini, eggplant, and the asparagus from the roasting pan, and continue to roast the red bell peppers for another 12–14 minutes.

3. **For Sauce:** To make the sauce, sauté the onion and garlic in olive oil in a medium sauce-pan over medium heat for 5 minutes. Add the red pepper flakes and oregano, stirring to coat, and sauté for another 2–3 minutes. Next, add the tomato paste and stir. Crush the whole canned tomatoes and add them, along with their juices, to the pan. Simmer on low for 16–20 minutes.

4. **To Complete:** Add a thin layer of the cooked sauce to the bottom of a 9" × 13" baking dish, and then add ¾ of the roasted zucchini slices, followed by a layer of eggplant, using ¾ of the eggplant slices. Next, layer half of the remaining sauce, ¼ cup of the chopped basil, the remainder of the zucchini and eggplant, all of the asparagus pieces and red bell peppers. Finish the layering with the remainder of the sauce and ¼ cup of basil. Cover with foil and bake at 375°F for 30 minutes, and then remove foil and cook another 30 minutes. Let it sit before cutting. Serve warm!

Red Hot Ratatouille

This all-too-easy, dazzling display of colorful vegetables is nothing short of delicious. Jalapeños and Sriracha sauce really know how to bring the heat! Turn up the temperature on this already seasoned and spiced medley of veggies by adding more jalapeños, a dash of cayenne, and a pinch of chipotle powder.

Serves 3–4

1 medium onion, thinly sliced
2 cloves garlic, chopped
1 tablespoon olive oil
2 large carrots, diced
1 cup water
½ red bell pepper, diced
½ green bell pepper, diced
10–12 mushrooms, sliced
2 large zucchini, cubed
2 small jalapeños, diced
1 (14-ounce) can diced
    tomatoes
1½ tablespoons Sriracha sauce
2 medium tomatoes, diced
Salt and pepper, to taste

1. In a large frying pan, cook the onion and garlic in olive oil over medium heat, and cook until slightly browned.

2. Add the carrots and water to the frying pan, cover, and simmer for 5–7 minutes.

3. Add the red and green peppers, mushrooms, zucchini, jalapeños, the can of tomatoes, and the Sriracha. Cover and simmer for about 15–20 minutes, or until all your vegetables are cooked.

4. Add the fresh tomatoes for additional flavor and cook for 2–3 more minutes.

5. Sprinkle with salt and pepper to taste, and serve as a side to an Italian-inspired poultry or beef dish, or enjoy it all by itself!

Hot and Spicy Stroganoff

This dish puts a pepped-up Paleo twist on a classic stroganoff recipe by featuring ground beef and mushrooms and a whole lot of spice! Fresh herbs like thyme and rosemary complement the heat of the cayenne-red pepper-Tabasco trio magnificently. This rich and succulent yet homey meal comes together in just minutes, but tastes like it took days to prepare. Serve over some Paleo pasta like spaghetti squash used in the Bolognese over Spaghetti Squash recipe, found later in this chapter, or over some Fiery Fried "Rice," found in Chapter 5. A little nutmeg and tarragon will add a nice lift to this spiced dish, so feel free to experiment!

1. In a skillet, melt the butter with the olive oil, and add the mushrooms and onion. Sauté until slightly softened and browned around the edges.

2. Add the browned ground beef to the pan, followed by the tomato paste, thyme, rosemary, cayenne, red pepper flakes, and garlic. Sauté for 3–4 minutes, then reduce heat to medium. Sprinkle arrowroot powder over meat mixture and stir until thoroughly combined, and then add the beef stock. The sauce will begin to thicken as it comes to a simmer. Reduce heat and simmer for about 4–5 minutes, then remove from heat and allow to cool.

3. Stir in the thick coconut cream and Tabasco. Sprinkle with salt and pepper, and serve over Spaghetti Squash (found in the Bolognese over Spaghetti Squash recipe), or over Fiery Fried "Rice" (see recipe in Chapter 5), or alongside a medley of roasted vegetables.

Serves 3–4

2 tablespoons clarified butter
1 tablespoon olive oil
8 ounces mushrooms, sliced
1 large onion, diced
1 pound lean ground beef, browned
2 tablespoons tomato paste
1½ teaspoons thyme
1½ teaspoons rosemary
1½ teaspoons cayenne pepper
½ teaspoon red pepper flakes
4 cloves garlic
1 tablespoon arrowroot powder
1¼ cups beef stock
⅔ cup thick coconut cream
2 tablespoons Tabasco sauce
Salt and pepper, to taste

Zesty Zucchini Boats

These creative, hollowed-out zucchini halves are filled with flavor and fiery fun! This versatile recipe can be made as a main dish or as a zesty appetizer for your next house party, and it is guaranteed to have your dinner guests all fired up! These Zesty Zucchini Boats are filled with a mixture of sautéed zucchini, garlic, and onions, and topped with a rich, creamy blend of almond yogurt, cilantro, and jalapeños. For a "meat-lovers" version, add slices of prepared peppered bacon, as a spiced pepperoni-like topping!

Serves 4

4 medium zucchini, halved lengthwise and hollowed out (remove ¾ of zucchini flesh, and set aside)

½ teaspoon salt, plus more to taste

½ teaspoon ground black pepper, plus more to taste

2 tablespoons coconut butter

1 medium sweet onion (or Vidalia), chopped

1 clove garlic, very finely chopped

⅓ cup dry arrowroot powder

1½ cups plain, unsweetened almond yogurt

Juice of ½ lime

2 jalapeños, seeded and chopped finely

2 tablespoons chopped cilantro

½ teaspoon garlic powder

1. Preheat the oven to 375°F. Season the zucchini cavities with salt and pepper, and arrange on a prepared baking sheet. Chop the flesh of the zucchini and set aside.

2. Heat the coconut butter in a skillet over medium heat. Add the onion and sauté until soft, about 2 minutes. Add the fresh garlic and continue cooking for 1 minute longer, then add the chopped zucchini flesh. Season the mixture with salt and pepper, and sauté until the zucchini is pale golden in color, about 3–4 minutes. Add the arrowroot powder, combine well, and cook for 1 additional minute, then remove from the heat.

3. In a small bowl, combine the yogurt, lime juice, jalapeños, cilantro, and garlic powder. Mix well until smooth and evenly combined.

4. Divide the sautéed zucchini between the hollowed "boats," then top with the yogurt mixture. Bake for 8–10 minutes, or until the boats are tender when pierced with a knife and the yogurt is bubbly and browned.

Bubbling Tomato Bake

This Bubbling Tomato Bake—a tasty, tangy, tomato dish with instantaneous mouthwatering effects—is sure to spice up your table! The cherry tomato halves are just bursting with flavor, having been roasted amongst a blend of savory herbs and spices, and will simply collapse under your fork. They are slightly tangy, but explode with a perfect balance of sweetness and spice. After a long day, this hot and spicy recipe only requires 10 minutes of prep time! Enjoy with some vino, and unwind while your taste buds go wild!

1. Preheat the oven to 325°F.

2. Layer the tomatoes in a glass baking dish and sprinkle the tomatoes with the minced shallot, sea salt, red pepper, and sliced jalapeños. Drizzle the canola oil and hot sauce on top.

3. Bake for 25–30 minutes, or until the desired doneness is achieved. Remove from heat, sprinkle with fresh basil, and serve.

Yields 3–4 servings

1 pound organic cherry tomatoes, halved
1 shallot, minced
¾ teaspoon sea salt
1 tablespoon red pepper flakes
2 jalapeños, sliced
2 tablespoons canola oil
2 tablespoons hot sauce
⅓ cup chopped basil

Chicken Cashew Curry

The cashews in this recipe add a sensational nutty flavor to this delicious curry. You can use raw or roasted cashews, and it is best to use unsalted nuts. If you prefer to use salted cashews, simply reduce the amount of salt called for in the recipe. In addition to the cashews, the powerful curry powder flavor is augmented by the blend of cumin, cayenne, turmeric, and red pepper flakes. Enjoy the heat!

Serves 4–6

For Coconut Rice:
1 head cauliflower, stem removed, roughly chopped
1 tablespoon coconut oil
Pinch salt
⅓ cup canned coconut milk
¼ cup unsweetened shredded coconut
1 teaspoon raw organic honey

For Chicken Cashew Curry:
1 tablespoon coconut oil
2 cloves garlic, minced
1 pound chicken, cut into cubes
⅔ cup canned coconut milk
½ cup puréed pumpkin
1 red onion, sliced
2–3 tablespoons curry powder
1 teaspoon cumin
½ teaspoon cayenne pepper
½ teaspoon turmeric
¼ teaspoon red pepper flakes
¼ teaspoon cinnamon
½ cup cashews
Salt and pepper, to taste
Cilantro, to garnish

1. **For Coconut Rice:** Place the chopped cauliflower in a food processor or blender with a shredding attachment to "rice" the cauliflower. Place a large pot over medium heat, add coconut oil, and then add the cauliflower. Add a pinch of salt, then cover, and stir occasionally. Add coconut milk, shredded coconut, and honey; cover and continue cooking, stirring occasionally to prevent burning. Allow the rice to cook for about 6–7 minutes, until the coconut milk has evaporated and the rice is "sticky." Spoon the rice into serving dishes.

2. **For Chicken Cashew Curry:** Place a large skillet over medium heat and add the other tablespoon of coconut oil. Add the garlic, followed by the chicken; after cooking the chicken a few minutes, add coconut milk and pumpkin and mix until the pumpkin breaks down. Next, add the sliced onion and spices and mix well. When chicken is finished cooking and the curry has thickened, remove from heat and add the cashews. Spoon the Chicken Cashew Curry over the "sticky" rice, add salt and pepper, and garnish with cilantro.

Sizzlin' Sweet Potato and Spinach Burrito

This beautiful blend of sweet and spice makes for a complete and satisfying meal, so enjoy this Paleo-style burrito any time of day! The bitter collard green leaves used here are a great replacement for the more traditional burrito wraps; they are just as sturdy and do not easily tear, they're super tasty, and they can be filled generously with hot or cold ingredients. The roasted cauliflower and sweet potato embrace the heat of the harissa (a blend of chili peppers, garlic, oil, and hot spices) marvelously in this recipe. Top these sensational sizzlers off with some Slow-Cooked Spicy Salsa (see Chapter 6) and a few slices of creamy avocado and bask in burrito bliss!

1. Preheat the oven to 400°F. Combine diced sweet potato and chopped cauliflower in a medium mixing bowl. Drizzle with 2 tablespoons of olive oil, harissa, salt, and pepper. Mix well, so harissa is evenly coating all the vegetables. Roast for 30 minutes.

2. While cauliflower and sweet potatoes are roasting, rinse the collard green leaves well and set aside to dry.

3. In a medium sauté pan, heat the remaining tablespoon of olive oil over medium heat. Add julienned pepper and sauté for about 7 minutes or until softened and starting to brown slightly. At this point, add the minced garlic, baby spinach leaves, a pinch of salt and pepper, and sauté until spinach starts to wilt, about 2 minutes. Remove from heat.

4. Remove cauliflower and sweet potatoes from oven and let cool for 1 minute. Split this mixture up between the 4 collard green leaves. Top each with the peppers, spinach, and salsa and roll the leaves up like a burrito. Make sure to tuck in the sides so none of this delicious filling drips out!

Serves 4

1 large sweet potato, diced
2 cups chopped cauliflower
3 tablespoons olive oil, divided use
2 tablespoons Homemade Harissa (see Chapter 5)
Salt and pepper, to taste
4 large collard green leaves (for burrito wrap)
1 red bell pepper, thinly julienned
1 teaspoon minced garlic
2 cups baby spinach
Slow-Cooked Spicy Salsa (see Chapter 6) and sliced avocados, optional, for garnish

Green Terrine with Zesty Pesto

Impress your friends and family at your next holiday party with this spicy vegetarian version of the popular French dish, terrine. This colorfully layered creation is nutrient-rich, with a variety of textures and flavors! The zesty pesto provides a creamy source of heat to the lightly seasoned vegetables. This dish is perfect for the intermediate chef looking to experiment with something new—and crank dinner up a notch!

Yields 1 loaf

For Zesty Pesto:
2 cups pine nuts
2 cups basil leaves
4 cloves garlic
Juice of 1–1½ lemons
1 teaspoon black pepper
¼–½ cup olive oil

For Green Terrine:
4 tablespoons olive oil, divided use
2 tablespoons minced garlic
½ teaspoon dried basil
½ teaspoon dried oregano
¼ teaspoon cayenne pepper
1 medium eggplant, sliced lengthwise into ¼" slices
2 large zucchini, sliced lengthwise into ¼" slices
2 large portobello mushroom caps
½ pound asparagus
2 shallots, diced
2 pounds spinach
Salt and pepper, to taste
1 (14-ounce) can fire-roasted diced tomatoes, drained
¼ cup tomato paste
1 tablespoon red pepper flakes

1. **For Zesty Pesto:** Combine all ingredients, except the olive oil, in a food processor. Blend together until well chopped. Purée, and add olive oil in small batches until the mixture starts to liquefy. Add olive oil until desired consistency is reached. This should make about 2–2½ cups of pesto.

2. **For Green Terrine:** Preheat the oven to 425°F. Whisk 3 tablespoons of olive oil, garlic, basil, oregano, and cayenne pepper in a small bowl. With a marinade brush, spread mixture evenly over the sliced eggplant, zucchini, mushroom caps, and asparagus. In a single layer, line vegetables on two foil-lined baking sheets. Bake vegetables for 30–45 minutes, turning occasionally, until softened. Remove from heat to cool.

3. While vegetables are roasting, heat remaining tablespoon of olive oil in a large sauté pan over medium heat. Add diced shallots and cook for about 5 minutes. Add spinach to pan and cook until wilted, about 5 minutes or less, stirring occasionally. Sprinkle with a pinch of salt and pepper and set aside to cool.

4. In a medium bowl, add diced tomatoes, tomato paste, and red pepper flakes. Mix until blended.

5. Line a 9" × 5" meatloaf pan with plastic wrap, leaving enough over the edges to cover the top of the terrine. Pack about ⅔ of the spinach/shallot mixture into the bottom and sides of the loaf pan. Line the sliced eggplant as the first layer on top of the spinach, follow with a thin layer of pesto and a scoop of the diced tomato mixture, and spread out. Add a layer of zucchini slices, followed by another thin layer of the pesto and diced tomatoes. Add a layer of asparagus, followed by more pesto and diced tomatoes. Layer the mushroom caps, topped with a thin layer of pesto and diced tomato mixture. Lastly, add the final layer of zucchini and top with the rest of the spinach to cover the top completely.

6. Once all the vegetables are snugly pressed into the loaf pan, cover with the extra plastic wrap. This loaf should be as tight as possible, so consider placing a heavy object on top to weigh the loaf down and keep it compact. Refrigerate overnight with a heavy object on top. Remove and pull back top layer of plastic wrap carefully. Invert loaf onto a large platter, and carefully pull off rest of the plastic wrap. Cut into 1" slices and serve cold.

Veggie Burgers with Fiery Fruit

These deliciously seasoned burgers topped with a light, citrus fruit salad will truly tantalize your taste buds! There is an explosion of flavor from the Sriracha in both the burgers and the fruit that provides a lingering heat. The sweet fruit salsa makes this meal a perfect option for a hot summer night, and is a great way to use up a smorgasbord of vegetables and fruit in your fridge.

Serves 4

1 head cauliflower, grated
2 large carrots, peeled and grated
3 tablespoons olive oil, divided use
1 medium onion, finely diced
2 jalapeños, seeded and diced
1 cup white mushrooms, diced
2 tablespoons minced garlic
½ cup sunflower seeds (ground in food processor, or finely chopped)
1 tablespoon Sriracha sauce
2 eggs
1 tablespoon almond flour
½ batch Fiery Fruit Salad (see Chapter 1)

1. Preheat the oven to 325°F. Mix grated cauliflower and carrots in a bowl with 1 tablespoon olive oil. Spread on a baking sheet and roast in the oven for about 30–45 minutes, mixing occasionally, until softened and starting to brown.

2. While cauliflower and carrots are roasting, add 1 tablespoon olive oil to a sauté pan over medium heat. Add diced onion and sauté for about 6 minutes, until translucent. Add diced jalapeños and mushrooms and sauté for another 6–7 minutes. Add garlic and sauté for another 2 minutes. Remove from heat.

3. Once all vegetables have cooled slightly, combine with all other ingredients (except the remaining 1 tablespoon oil) in large mixing bowl. Incorporate all ingredients together with hands, and form 4 large patties. For a more solid veggie burger, refrigerate for 15–30 minutes before cooking.

4. In a large pan, add remaining tablespoon of olive oil over medium-high heat. Add veggie burgers to pan and fry for about 6 minutes on both sides until browned.

5. Take ½ of the Fiery Fruit recipe and add to food processor. Pulse until fruit is chopped, creating a salsa-like consistency. Serve on top of warm burgers.

Lethal Latkes

Latkes are a traditional type of "potato pancake," frequently served during the Jewish holiday Hanukkah. This Paleo spin-off mixes sweet with spice and creates a deliciously filling meal! The cumin and chili powder accent the jalapeño in this recipe, and blend perfectly with the sugary flavor of sweet potato and coconut flour.

1. Combine all ingredients, except the coconut oil, in a large mixing bowl. Stir until well blended. This should be a sticky, batter-like mixture that sticks well when the latke is formed.

2. Heat coconut oil in large nonstick skillet until melted. Add ⅓ cup size spoonfuls of mixture to skillet, and pat down slightly. Fry on one side for about 5–7 minutes, until browned, and flip. Fry on the other side until browned. Fry in batches.

3. Remove from heat and serve warm. If making in advance, refrigerate until serving. Heat in the oven for about 10 minutes before serving, if chilled.

Yields 12 latkes

3 cups grated sweet potato
3 chives, finely chopped
1 teaspoon minced garlic
1 jalapeño, seeded and diced
½ teaspoon cumin
½ teaspoon chili powder
1 tablespoon chopped cilantro
2 eggs
1½ tablespoons coconut flour
2 tablespoons coconut oil

🔥 TOP THAT!

Latkes that are served as a meal typically have a topping for added taste and texture. These particular latkes have more of a savory flavor, and are simply delicious when topped with slices of smoked salmon. Be creative! Try topping them off with spicy mustard, sautéed spinach, or even the zesty pesto found in the recipe for Green Terrine with Zesty Pesto, found in this chapter!

Eggplant Rollatini

This delicious Italian dinner dish is usually covered and/or filled with a blend of different cheeses. This Paleo version incorporates the same satisfying taste, but without the dairy! The spicy sausage and vegetable filling, wrapped in thin "breaded" eggplant, create a deliciously irresistible, well-rounded meal. These fiery Eggplant Rollatinis pair perfectly with a side salad or even with a side of roasted spaghetti squash topped with a spicy marinara!

Serves 3

2 eggs
1½ cups coconut flour
Pinch salt and pepper
1 large eggplant, thinly sliced using a mandoline
3 tablespoons olive oil, divided use
1 small onion, diced
1 cup chopped white mushrooms
½ pound ground spicy sausage meat
Sliced basil, for garnish
Fiery Marinara (see Bison Meatballs and Fiery Marinara recipe in Chapter 2)

1. Preheat the oven to 350°F. Crack both eggs and whisk in a large, flat bowl. Place coconut flour, salt, and pepper in a separate large, flat bowl. Once the entire eggplant is sliced with a mandoline, dip a piece into the coconut flour, and then into the egg mixture, and back into the coconut flour. Repeat this step with all of the eggplant slices. You may need more egg and/or coconut flour for this process depending on the size of the eggplant.

2. Pour 1 tablespoon olive oil into a medium skillet over medium heat. Add onion and mushrooms and sauté for 5 minutes. Add the spicy ground sausage to the skillet and sauté until cooked through. Set aside.

3. In a large skillet, add remaining 2 tablespoons of olive oil and heat over medium-high heat. Fry (in batches) each slice of eggplant in the skillet, about 2–3 minutes per side (to get a bit of a crust).

4. Once all eggplant pieces have been fried, start filling each slice with the sausage mixture and roll into cylinders. Carefully place into a lightly oiled baking dish and top with the Fiery Marinara. Bake for about 20 minutes. Enjoy hot with fresh basil as a garnish.

Zippy Zucchini Bake

This versatile Zippy Zucchini Bake can be served at breakfast, brunch, lunch, or dinner and is a great way of incorporating zucchini and other vegetables into a meal! It's super easy to make this dish ahead of time, and it can be stored in the refrigerator for about a week. The poblano peppers, also referred to as ancho chilies when dried, used in this recipe are mild and very tolerable, and can be swapped out for jalapeños or serrano peppers, if you prefer to turn up the heat!

1. Preheat the oven to 350°F. In a large oven-proof skillet, heat olive oil over medium-high heat. Add onion and poblano peppers and sauté for 5–7 minutes, until softened. Turn heat down slightly and add zucchini, sofrito, garlic, cooked sausage, chili powder, and coriander. Stir together and sauté for another 5 minutes, so flavors can blend.

2. Meanwhile, whisk eggs, salt, and pepper in a large mixing bowl until well blended. Add egg mixture to the skillet and stir so all ingredients are incorporated.

3. Place skillet in oven and bake for 35–45 minutes, or until eggs are set and the top starts to turn gold. If you do not have an oven-proof skillet, transfer all ingredients to a lightly oiled baking dish and bake for the same amount of time.

Serves 6–8

1 tablespoon olive oil
1 medium onion, diced
2 poblano peppers, seeded and diced
2 zucchini, sliced into ¼" rounds
3 tablespoons sofrito
1 teaspoon minced garlic
2 cups ground sausage, cooked
1 teaspoon chili powder
½ teaspoon ground coriander
8 large eggs
Salt and pepper, to taste

🔥 **SPICY SOFRITO!**

Sofrito is a type of pepper-based sauce, widely used to flavor food in Latin American cuisine. It is a condensed, relish-like ingredient made up of finely chopped and blended peppers, onions, tomatoes, garlic, and spices. These ingredients are braised in cooking oils and jarred. You can find this at any grocery store, and use it in hot or cold foods.

Ground Turkey–Stuffed Peppers

There's nothing more versatile than these Ground Turkey–Stuffed peppers! Add ground chicken, beef, pork, or even veal to up the amount of protein in this dish; enjoy the peppers over a bed of dark, leafy greens and a variety of different colored tomatoes; or make this spicy recipe even hotter by experimenting with various fiery spices and fresh herbs like cayenne, crushed red pepper flakes, and ground chipotle peppers! A hot sauce like Tabasco would ramp up the heat even more. Drizzle it over the finished product, and/or add it to the ground beef while browning.

Serves 4

1 pound lean ground turkey
1 medium onion, chopped
2 cloves garlic, chopped
1 zucchini, chopped
1 (14-ounce) can diced tomatoes, drained
½ teaspoon cumin
½ teaspoon chili powder
Pinch of pepper
2 eggs
4 medium bell peppers

1. Preheat the oven to 375°F. Brown meat in large skillet over medium-high heat, breaking up as it cooks, about 8 minutes. Add onion and garlic, and cook 4 minutes. Add zucchini and cook another 3 minutes. Remove from heat, add tomatoes, spices, and eggs. Mix well.

2. Cut tops off peppers and scoop out the seeds. Spoon the meat mixture into peppers. Stand the peppers up in a baking dish, and place the extra meat mixture in a second baking dish.

3. Bake for 30–40 minutes until well heated and peppers are slightly browned. Remove from the oven and serve warm.

Bolognese over Spaghetti Squash

Spaghetti squash is versatile and delicious, so be daring with fiery additions to the Bolognese like hot sauce and jalapeños. The Chipotle Tomato Sauce or Jalapeño Tomatillo Sauce, both from Chapter 2, would work well as the sauce in this recipe, if you'd prefer to make it a purely vegetarian dish. If you're a meat lover, try a variety of (or combination of) other ground meats like veal, chicken, or even bison.

1. **For Spaghetti Squash:** Preheat the oven to 375°F. Pierce squash multiple times with a sharp knife. Place on a pan and roast for approximately 60–75 minutes.

2. Turn squash over halfway through. After roasted squash has cooled, cut it in half lengthwise and scoop out the seeds. Scrape squash with a fork to remove flesh in long strands (like "spaghetti").

3. **For Bolognese:** Heat canola oil in a heavy pan over medium heat. Add in garlic, onion, carrot, and celery. Cook 5–10 minutes or until soft. Season with pepper and crushed red pepper flakes. Add meat to pot and break apart with a spoon until cooked through, about 8–10 minutes. Stir in coconut milk and bring to a simmer for about 10 minutes. Stir in wine and continue to simmer for 10 more minutes. Add in chopped tomatoes and basil. Let simmer for up to 1 hour.

4. **To Complete:** Top spaghetti squash with the Bolognese and mix until evenly combined. Transfer to 4–6 individual serving bowls. Serve warm!

Serves 4–6

For Spaghetti Squash:
1 spaghetti squash

For Bolognese:
1 tablespoon canola oil
1 clove garlic, finely chopped
½ yellow onion, finely chopped
1 carrot, finely chopped
2 celery stalks, finely chopped
½ teaspoon pepper
¼–½ teaspoon crushed red pepper flakes
16 ounces ground meat (free-range beef is recommended)
½ cup coconut milk
½ cup Italian red wine
1 (28-ounce) can chopped or puréed tomatoes (look for tomatoes only, no added salt or sugar)
⅛ cup finely chopped basil

Wasabi-Crusted Tuna

This Wasabi-Crusted Tuna provides loads of heart-healthy omega-3 fatty acids and can also be served as a first course when sliced into smaller pieces. The wasabi plant is part of the same family as horseradish and mustard seed, and has an extremely strong flavor known to stimulate the nasal passages. Wasabi's powerful pungency never fails to create that *wow* factor! Serve over a bed of stir-fried spinach or baby bok choy.

Serves 2–4

2 (1"-thick) tuna steaks
1 egg
1 cup coconut or almond milk
5 ounces wasabi peas
1 cup almond flour
3 tablespoons canola oil

1. Slice each tuna steak in half; wash and dry each one and wrap tightly in plastic wrap. Place in the freezer for 45 minutes.

2. Mix the egg and milk together, and set aside. Crush the wasabi peas until coarsely ground. Unwrap the tuna, coat each piece in flour, then dip into the egg and milk mixture, and then roll in the crushed wasabi, coating each side. Allow tuna to sit for 10–15 minutes, while preheating a heavy frying pan over low heat.

3. Add canola oil and turn frying pan up to high. Add tuna after 1 minute. Sauté tuna 1 minute on all sides. Serve immediately as tuna steaks, or slice into multiple smaller pieces.

🔥 WHAT'S UP WITH WASABI?

Wasabi is a member of the same family as cabbage, mustard, and horseradish. It has an intense flavor, which originates from the root and results in the powerful stimulation of the nasal passages. Covering prepared wasabi helps preserve its flavor, which is quickly minimized if left uncovered for too long.

Pepper-Crusted Steak

This hot and spicy Pepper-Crusted Steak is a simple recipe that is both easy to prepare and guaranteed to melt in your mouth! The wonderful, smoky flavors created by the seared peppercorns are simply staggering. This fiery dish includes black and green peppercorns that, once crushed, release essential oils with pungent flavors. When the crushed peppercorns combine with the beef, a perfect pair is made! Enjoy with a variety of your favorite veggies!

1. Place the peppercorns in a sealed plastic bag. Using a mallet, break them into small pieces (do not pulverize). Add them to a mixing bowl, add coconut butter, and mix together.

2. Season the steaks on both sides with fresh herbs and spices, and then rub peppercorns on the steaks, coating all sides.

3. Heat canola oil for about 3 minutes in a frying pan over medium heat. Cook steaks evenly on both sides (4 minutes per side, for medium-rare). Remove from heat and allow to sit for 5 minutes before serving.

Serves 4

1 tablespoon whole black peppercorns

1 tablespoon whole green peppercorns

2 tablespoons coconut butter, slightly softened

4 (6-ounce) lean cuts of steak (filet mignon or sirloin is recommended), about 1½" thick

Fresh herbs and spices, as desired

2 tablespoons canola oil

Seafood Fra Diavolo

A fiery dish traditionally served over pasta, this recipe can be easily tailored to meet all the needs of your Paleo palate. The sauce has a thick consistency, which means you can serve it without pasta, and the hot and spicy cayenne, red pepper, and chili powder trio simply work wonders. Enjoy!

Serves 2–3

1 filleted fish of choice (a white fish with a tougher skin is recommended)
3 tablespoons coconut butter
2 tablespoons extra-virgin olive oil
6 cloves garlic, chopped
½ teaspoon cayenne pepper
½ teaspoon red pepper flakes
½ teaspoon chili powder
Black pepper and sea salt, to taste
1 (28-ounce) can roasted tomatoes
1 pound raw shrimp, peeled and deveined
2 tablespoons fresh flat leaf parsley (chopped)
1 tablespoon lemon zest

1. Preheat a cast-iron grill pan over medium heat, and when it is hot, place the white fish in the pan, skin side down. Grill until the skin side is really crunchy. Note: The flesh should remain soft (but cooked).

2. Melt the butter and oil in a deep saucepan, and add the chopped garlic, cooking until the garlic turns golden brown, and then add the spices. Add the tomatoes and simmer on low for 15 minutes. Add the shrimp and mix well, then add the parsley and lemon zest. Cook for another 5–10 minutes, until the shrimp are fully cooked.

3. Chop the cooked white fish into small pieces, but keep separate from sauce. Upon serving, ladle the shrimp and sauce into a bowl, adding a few pieces of the white fish on top, skin side down.

Spicy Chicken Cashew Stir Fry

This fiery Spicy Chicken Cashew Stir Fry is such an enjoyable, aromatic, and decadent dish. It's packed full of color, fiery flavors, and fun! The cashew butter combined with the variety of seasonings creates a truly unforgettable treat. Build on the spice of the hot sauce, ginger, and cilantro, and kick this dish up a notch with some red pepper and minced jalapeño. Eliminate the chicken from the recipe if a vegetarian version is desired.

1. Using two separate frying pans, add the chicken and ½ tablespoon coconut oil to one, and cook over low-medium heat. Add 1 tablespoon of coconut oil, garlic, and the vegetables to the second pan, also cooking over low-medium heat.

2. After 1–2 minutes of cooking, add the coconut aminos, hot sauce, cilantro, ginger, cashews, and cashew butter to the vegetable pan. Stir until evenly combined.

3. Once the chicken is cooked through (though not overcooked on the outside), add to the vegetable pan. Next, add the egg on top of everything, and stir until the egg is fully cooked. Serve immediately.

Serves 2–3

2 chicken breasts, sliced into pieces
1½ tablespoons coconut oil, divided use
½ tablespoon minced garlic
3 cups mixed vegetable medley (broccoli, carrots, snap peas, onions, peppers, etc.), chopped
4 tablespoons coconut aminos
1½ tablespoons hot sauce
¼ cup cilantro, diced
2 tablespoons ginger, diced
¼ cup cashews, chopped
1½ tablespoons cashew butter
1 egg

Roasted Buffalo Shrimp

This much healthier, lower-calorie version of hot and spicy buffalo chicken pairs well atop a large dinner salad, or alongside some grilled leafy greens, or even intertwined among a kebab of grilled vegetables. These shrimp also make an excellent start to a casual dinner party as a tasty dipping appetizer with a fiery kick!

Yields 3 entrée-size servings (or 8–9 appetizer-size servings)

For Buffalo Shrimp:
2 tablespoons finely grated lemon zest
2 cloves garlic, minced
¾ teaspoon celery seeds
2½ teaspoons sweet paprika
¼ teaspoon cayenne pepper
¼ teaspoon sea salt
2 tablespoons raw organic honey
¼ cup extra-virgin olive oil
1½ pounds large shrimp, peeled (except for the tails) and deveined

For Dipping Sauce:
2 tablespoons fresh lemon juice
1 cup coconut milk, chilled
¼ cup celery leaves, finely chopped
¼ teaspoon sea salt

1. **For Buffalo Shrimp:** Place 2 rimmed baking sheets in the oven, and preheat to 450°F. In a large bowl, combine lemon zest, garlic, celery seeds, paprika, cayenne pepper, ¼ teaspoon sea salt, honey, and olive oil. Add the shrimp to the bowl, and mix well until evenly coated. Place the coated shrimp on the hot pans in a single layer. Roast for about 5 minutes, or until the bottoms are browned and shrimp are opaque throughout. Do not flip the shrimp.

2. **For Dipping Sauce:** Mix the lemon juice, chilled coconut milk, celery leaves, and sea salt, and stir until evenly combined. Serve alongside or drizzled on top of the cooked shrimp.

Chipotle Chicken Casserole

A smoking-hot, blazing concoction, this Chipotle Chicken Casserole is guaranteed to impress even the most daring spicy food lovers. The chili, chipotle powder, and crushed red pepper combination add a serious "wow" factor to an otherwise simple dish. The cumin and cilantro bring a little more pep, intensifying the heat to a perfect degree of H-O-T!

1. Preheat the oven to 375°F.

2. Sauté red pepper pieces in olive oil in a medium skillet over medium heat for 3–4 minutes; add green onions and garlic, and continue sautéing for 2–3 more minutes.

3. Cut cauliflower florets into ½ –1" chunks, place in a large bowl, and add chili and chipotle powders, crushed red pepper flakes, and cumin; and mix until well blended. Stir in red pepper concoction, chicken, tomatoes, and cilantro, and pour entire mixture into a pre-greased casserole dish. Bake for 20–30 minutes.

Serves 2–4

1 red bell pepper, chopped
Olive oil, for sautéing
1 cup green onions, chopped
3 cloves garlic, minced
1 large head cauliflower, cut into florets and steamed
1 teaspoon chili powder
1 teaspoon chipotle powder
1 teaspoon crushed red pepper flakes
½ teaspoon ground cumin
2 grilled chicken breasts, chopped
1 cup cherry tomatoes, chopped
3 tablespoons cilantro, chopped

Beef and Squash Pot Pie

In this spicy, sensational dish, the sweetness of the butternut squash accentuates the succulent, savory spices underneath. Go ahead and use whatever veggies you have lying around; this is a very versatile recipe. Carrots, green and red bell peppers, and spinach are recommended, but use your imagination! This recipe is a delicious way to utilize an array of leftover vegetables.

Serves 2–4

1½ pounds butternut squash, peeled, seeded, and cubed
½ onion, diced
3 tablespoons coconut oil, divided use
2 carrots, peeled and chopped
1 pound ground beef
1 teaspoon dried thyme
½ teaspoon sea salt
½ teaspoon cumin
½ teaspoon black pepper
¼ teaspoon ground cayenne pepper
½ green bell pepper, chopped
½ red bell pepper, chopped
1 cup chopped frozen spinach

1. Place squash in a medium sauce pot and cover with water. Boil squash over medium heat for 20–30 minutes, until soft. Remove from heat, drain squash, and set aside.

2. Sauté onion in 1 tablespoon coconut oil in a cast-iron skillet over medium heat for 8–10 minutes, then add the carrots and cook for another 6–9 minutes until soft. Add the ground beef and continue sautéing until meat is no longer pink, separating it into crumbles while it cooks. Add the thyme, sea salt, cumin, black and cayenne pepper, peppers, and spinach, and cook another 3–5 minutes.

3. Mash the butternut squash (with a hand mixer, blender, or food processor) with 2 tablespoons coconut oil, until smooth.

4. Transfer the beef and vegetable mixture to a 9" × 13" baking dish and add the mashed squash on top, distributing evenly; heat for just a few minutes at 375°F, and serve warm.

Spicy Chicken Tacos with Cauliflower Tortillas

The chicken breast used in this super spicy dish becomes incredibly flavorful after slowly simmering in a blend of savory seasonings. This dish is simple; it uses taco seasoning and salsa, but there is plenty of room for creativity here! Try adding a little hot sauce, and a red-black-cayenne pepper trio for a more powerful degree of spice. This recipe calls for a cauliflower tortilla, but feel free to try this dish with the Coconut Flour Tortillas found in the recipe for Spicy Beef Tacos with Coconut Flour Tortillas in this chapter.

1. **For Chicken Taco Filling:** Heat olive oil in a large skillet over medium-high heat. Add chicken and cook through, then stir in the taco seasoning, water, and salsa, and continue cooking for 8–10 minutes.

2. **For Cauliflower Tortillas:** Preheat the oven to 375°F and microwave cauliflower for 5–7 minutes, stirring halfway through. Place the the cooked cauliflower in a large dish towel or other permeable cloth and drain all excess water from the cauliflower. Combine the drained cauliflower and eggs, mixing until smooth, and then place the mixture on a baking sheet(s), in ¼"-thick circles. Bake for 10 minutes, flip, and continue baking for another 6–8 minutes until tortillas have dried out. Transfer to a cooling rack.

3. **To Complete:** Assemble tacos using any combination of toppings and serve.

Yields 4–6 tacos

For Chicken Taco Filling:
1 pound boneless chicken breast, chopped
1 tablespoon olive oil
2 tablespoons taco seasoning
½ cup water
½ cup salsa (jarred or homemade, see Slow-Cooked Spicy Salsa in Chapter 6)

For Cauliflower Tortillas:
Florets from 2 heads of cauliflower, processed or hand grated into a crumb-like texture
6 eggs *or* 8 egg whites

To Complete (amounts as desired):
Lettuce, shredded
Guacamole
Salsa
Sautéed peppers and onions

Spicy Beef Tacos with Coconut Flour Tortillas

Use your culinary imagination for the toppings in this dish! Prepare with the same topping ingredients listed in the Spicy Chicken Taco recipe found in this chapter, or be wild and experiment with some banana peppers, olives, jalapeños, or even a few chilies. Amplify the spiciness here by adding ground chipotle peppers to really blast the heat!

Yields 4–6 tacos

Beef Taco Filling:
2 cloves garlic, minced
1 pound lean ground beef
1½ teaspoons black pepper
1½ teaspoons ground cumin
1½ teaspoons ground coriander
½ teaspoon paprika
1½ cups canned diced tomatoes
 (with green chilies)

Coconut Flour Tortillas:
½ cup coconut flour
½ teaspoon baking powder
¼ teaspoon salt
1½ cups egg whites
¾ cup almond or coconut milk

1. **For Beef Taco Filling:** Warm garlic in a skillet over medium-high heat, then add the beef and cook until browned, breaking beef into crumbles as it cooks, about 8–10 minutes. Stir in the spices and tomatoes, cooking until most of the liquid is absorbed.

2. **For Coconut Flour Tortillas:** Mix together the coconut flour, baking powder, salt, egg whites, and milk, and set aside for 10 minutes. Stir again and add ¼ cup of the mixture to a skillet, distributing liquid evenly in pan, and cook over medium-high heat for about 1–2 minutes, until it is ready to flip. Continue cooking another 1–2 minutes and remove from pan once cooked. Repeat with the remaining tortilla batter.

3. **To Complete:** To assemble, fill each Coconut Flour Tortilla with some ground beef taco filling. Roll to seal, and enjoy!

🔥 PREFER A SIMPLER VERSION?

If you want to simplify this recipe, just substitute fresh salsa and taco seasoning for the diced tomatoes and individual spices in this recipe. The tortillas used in this dish can also be concocted using almond flour, or cauliflower, like the Spicy Chicken Tacos with Cauliflower Tortillas (see recipe in this chapter).

Spiced Salmon with Salsa

This Spiced Salmon with Salsa is a delicious, sweet, and spicy dish that can be completed in less than 30 minutes, yet it tastes like it required hours of preparation. Mango salsa is included here, though a variety of salsa flavors will work too. For example, the Slow-Cooked Spicy Salsa from Chapter 6 would be a super spiced-up substitute! The cilantro, jalapeño, and Mexican hot sauce deserve all the credit for torquing up the heat in this recipe—increase the hot ingredients to make it even more of a scorcher!

1. **For Mango Salsa:** Stir together the mango, pepper, onion, cilantro, lime juice, honey, and jalapeño, and refrigerate until needed.

2. **For Spiced Salmon:** Combine honey, hot sauce, and lime juice and brush evenly over salmon fillets. Place salmon (flesh side down) on a grill (sprayed thoroughly with cooking spray) over medium coals, and cook 2–3 minutes until lightly blackened. Flip and cook for another 8–10 minutes, reapplying sauce as needed. Once cooked, remove from heat and top with prepared mango salsa.

Serves 4–6

For Mango Salsa:
1 large mango, peeled and diced
¼ cup red bell pepper, finely chopped
¼ cup red onion, finely chopped
2 tablespoons cilantro, chopped
1 tablespoon fresh lime juice
1 tablespoon raw organic honey
1 small jalapeño, seeded and minced

For Spiced Salmon:
⅓ cup raw organic honey
2 tablespoons Mexican hot sauce
1 tablespoon fresh lime juice
4 (6-ounce) salmon fillets, rinsed and patted dry

Zesty Paleo Meatloaf

A Paleo-approved comfort food, this Zesty Paleo Meatloaf is sure to warm you up from the inside out! Enjoy atop some mashed or riced cauliflower, or a medley of roasted root veggies. The rice and succulent flavor of the beef and pork/veal blend is accented beautifully with a blend of veggies, savory seasonings, and a sensational spicy marinade!

Serves 8

For Meatloaf Marinade:

15 ounces tomato sauce (canned or homemade)

6 ounces tomato paste

3 tablespoons spicy mustard

2 tablespoons lime juice

For Meatloaf:

1½ pounds lean ground beef

1½ pounds lean ground pork or veal

2 eggs

1 cup chopped onion (yellow is recommended)

1 cup shredded carrots

1 cup chopped tomatoes

1 cup chopped green and red bell peppers

½ cup arrowroot powder

½ teaspoon cayenne pepper

½ teaspoon cumin

Salt and pepper, to taste

1. **For Meatloaf Marinade:** Stir together all marinade ingredients, until thoroughly combined.

2. **For Meatloaf:** Preheat the oven to 375°F. Mix together all of the loaf ingredients, combining evenly. Form a loaf in a roasting pan and bake for 40–50 minutes. Remove loaf from oven, and turn heat up to 450°F. Evenly coat the meatloaf with the marinade, until all sides are covered, and return to the oven for about 15 minutes, until sauce has thickened.

Racy Rub Roast

This hearty roast of spiced beef is absolutely phenomenal, and practically foolproof! The deeply flavored, seven-spice dry rub is simply extraordinary, and perfectly augments the beef's natural body and character, creating a beautiful and elegant dinner party recipe that is absolutely sure to please even your toughest of critics! Serve alongside a rich vegetable dish like the Harvest Spinach and Sprouts, found in Chapter 5.

1. In a bowl, mix together all ingredients, except for the roast and canola oil, and then rub all over the beef, coating evenly. Refrigerate overnight, uncovered.

2. Preheat the oven to 350°F and heat oil in a large frying pan over medium heat. Brown the roast on both sides, about 2 minutes each side. Place the roast in a large roasting pan, on a wire rack. Transfer the roast to the oven, cooking until the center reaches 125°F. Remove from heat and set aside for 20 minutes before slicing and serving.

Serves 5–6

2 teaspoons salt
1 teaspoon coriander
1 teaspoon paprika
1 teaspoon ground cumin
1 teaspoon ground black pepper
¾ teaspoon unsweetened cocoa powder
¼ teaspoon allspice
1 (2–3 pound) beef roast
1 tablespoon canola oil

Savory Salmon Curry

Want this dish mild or super spiced-up? The choice is yours! That is the beauty of this sensational savory salmon. The ginger and garlic boost the delightful scent of the spicy curry, and linger deliciously for hours after you prepare this divine dish. A little sweetness from the honey and cinnamon complement the savory flavors wonderfully!

Serves 4

4 salmon fillets
1½ tablespoons canola oil
1½ teaspoons garam masala
1 teaspoon raw organic honey
½ teaspoon cinnamon
½ teaspoon ground ginger
¼ teaspoon garlic powder

1. Preheat the oven to 450°F. Prepare a baking pan with cooking spray, and add the salmon fillets.

2. Combine all other ingredients, mixing until evenly combined. Coat mixture evenly over salmon fillets, and bake until the fish is flaky when touched with a fork, about 15 minutes.

Spicy Sausage Bolognese over Zucchini Spaghetti

Bolognese is a thick, meaty comfort food that tastes great atop anything! This spiced-up version will warm your body up from the inside out and provide a ton of protein to give you a long-lasting full feeling. The zucchini "spaghetti" is a wonderful base for this dish. It holds up to the heat and heaviness of the sauce and absorbs the spice from the garlic, red pepper flakes, and paprika. You will not be able to resist seconds when you try this filling dinner option!

1. **For Spicy Sausage Bolognese:** Purée tomatoes, garlic, thyme, red pepper flakes, and paprika in a blender or processor and set aside. Heat oil in a large skillet over medium-high heat and add the sausage, cooking until browned (about 10 minutes). Stir the sausage meat while cooking, allowing the meat to break apart evenly. Add the tomato mixture to the sausage pan, and bring the combination to a boil. Continue cooking, and stirring periodically, for about 10 minutes, until the sauce has thickened, and then stir in the coconut butter.

2. **For Zucchini Pasta:** Using a julienne peeler, finely peel zucchini into thin strands. Add lemon juice and mix, followed by the the onion and garlic, and finally the salt, pepper, and oregano. Top generously with warm Bolognese sauce.

Serves 4

For Spicy Sausage Bolognese:

1 (28-ounce) can whole tomatoes in juice
5 cloves garlic, minced
1 teaspoon dried thyme
½ teaspoon crushed red pepper flakes
½ teaspoon paprika
2 tablespoons olive oil
1 pound hot Italian sausage, casings removed
¼ cup coconut butter

For Zucchini Pasta:

2 large zucchini
2 lemons, juiced
3 tablespoons minced onion
1 teaspoon minced garlic
¼ teaspoon sea salt
¼ teaspoon ground black pepper
¼ teaspoon oregano

Spicy Mango Mahi-Mahi

A classic mango chutney calls for added sugar, but in this delectable dish, the ripe mango adds just the right amount of sweet flavor. This mango chutney also packs a powerfully flavorful, slightly pungent punch, highlighting the taste of the fiery jalapeño, cilantro, and pepper combination.

Serves 2

1 teaspoon olive oil

1½ tablespoons lime juice, divided use

½ teaspoon sea salt, divided use

¼ teaspoon ground pepper

2 (4-ounce) mahi-mahi fillets

1 large ripe mango, peeled, pitted, and diced

2 green onions, thinly sliced

1 tablespoon diced jalapeño

1 tablespoon cilantro

1. Mix olive oil, 1 teaspoon lime juice, ¼ teaspoon sea salt, and ground pepper and evenly coat the fish fillets. Preheat the grill to high.

2. Combine mango, green onions, jalapeño, cilantro, and the remaining lime juice and sea salt. Mix well and set aside.

3. Place mahi-mahi fillets on grill, top side down, reduce heat to medium, and close cover for 2–3 minutes. Once the outer edges of the fish appear cooked, flip and grill another 2–4 minutes until done, and then remove from heat.

4. Add mango topping to the fish and serve immediately.

Pulled Pork Picante

An absolute breeze in a slow cooker, this pepped-up pork dish guarantees super satisfying results! The minced chipotle pepper is the key ingredient here, so go ahead and add more if you prefer it hotter. The moist, tender, fall-off-the-bone pork is a real winner. Ready in just 6 hours, it will be a joy to arrive home to this Paleo–palate pleaser after a long, hard day.

1. Combine onion, oregano, bay leaves, chipotle, adobo sauce, tomatoes, salt, and pepper in a 5-quart slow cooker. Add pork shoulder, and mix all ingredients well. Cover and cook on high for 6 hours.

2. Remove pork from slow cooker and shred meat with a fork. Place shredded pork back into the slow cooker and mix with sauce. Discard bay leaves and serve warm.

Serves 8

1 medium onion, diced
1 teaspoon dried oregano
2 dried bay leaves
1 chipotle in adobo, minced
1 tablespoon adobo sauce
1 (28-ounce) can crushed
 tomatoes
1 (14.5-ounce) can whole
 tomatoes in purée
2 teaspoons sea salt
½ teaspoon ground pepper
3 pounds boneless pork shoulder, trimmed and halved

Jalapeño Chicken Burgers

Beef up your next burger with these juicy ground chicken patties, stuffed with onion, garlic, jalapeño, and a spicy blend of fresh cilantro, cumin, paprika, and red pepper. Cool down with a dollop of cold, creamy guacamole. Ground turkey will substitute seamlessly for the ground chicken here if you'd like a little variation.

Serves 8

3 pounds lean ground chicken
   or turkey
1½ cups diced onion
½ cup chopped cilantro
4 cloves garlic, minced
1 diced jalapeño
2 teaspoons dried cumin
2 teaspoons dried paprika
2 teaspoons red pepper flakes

1. Combine all ingredients in a large bowl, and mix well until evenly combined.

2. Form 8 patties and grill over medium-high heat for about 10–12 minutes, flipping halfway through. The burgers are fully cooked once their internal temperatures reach 170°F.

Grilled Jerk Pork Loin

A mouthwatering, crowd-pleasing twist on pork, this Grilled Jerk Pork Loin is guaranteed to have everyone coming back for more! With a blazing blend of fiery flavor, the habanero peppers initiate the heat, and the intricate combination of herbs and spices keep the fire roaring. Pair with the similarly seasoned Jerk-Inspired Collard Greens or Stir-Fried Gingered Asparagus recipes, both found in Chapter 5.

1. In a blender or food processor, blend the peppers, onions, ginger, and garlic until fine, then add the cider, lime juice, coconut aminos, olive oil, and honey and mix well. Finish with the remaining herbs and spices and blend until smooth.

2. Coat the pork tenderloin with the above mixture in a casserole dish, and massage marinade into the meat until evenly coated. Cover and refrigerate 10–12 hours.

3. Preheat a lightly oiled grill on medium-high heat and grill pork over the hot coals, turning periodically to produce even browning on all sides. Cook until the internal temperature reaches 145°F, then remove from heat and slice into thin pieces to serve.

Serves 8–10

2 habanero peppers, seeded
1½ cups chopped green onion
1 small yellow onion, chopped
1 piece fresh ginger, peeled and thinly sliced
3 cloves garlic, peeled
¼ cup apple cider
¼ cup lime juice
3 tablespoons coconut aminos
3 tablespoons olive oil
2 tablespoons raw organic honey
1 tablespoon dried thyme
1 tablespoon ground allspice
1 tablespoon sea salt
1½ teaspoons black pepper
1½ teaspoons mustard seed
1½ teaspoons ground nutmeg
1 teaspoon ground cinnamon
½ teaspoon cayenne pepper
3 pounds butterflied pork tenderloin, pounded

CHAPTER 5
Sides

Side dishes play a key role in defining a meal, and these hot and spicy sides will keep mealtime interesting! The main entrée in traditional American fare is served with two side dishes, which most often include a vegetable and a starch (like a potato or rice, or a pasta dish). However, these common starches don't fit in with the Paleo lifestyle. You might assume that Paleo sides may get a little boring, but every single recipe in this chapter—from the Zesty Zucchini Chips to the Spicy Sweet Potato Mash to the Stir-Fried Gingered Asparagus—is sure to debunk this assumption! Hot paprika, cayenne pepper, and hot chili flakes are just a few of the ingredients used in these next recipes to add a little kick and amp up just about any main entrée.

Autumnal Acorn Squash, Spicily Stuffed

This delicious fall-themed side dish incorporates a ton of flavor and texture for your taste buds! The fruit baked inside the squash caramelizes and creates a sweet canvas for the cardamom and allspice. This dish has a fragrant peppery flavor, and will make your house smell amazing! It is warming inside and out and will impress your guests at your next holiday party.

Serves 4

1 large egg
1 cup Fiery Fried "Rice" (see recipe in this chapter)
½ cup peeled chopped apple (preferably tart)
½ cup chopped cranberries
½ cup chopped celery
2 jalapeños, finely chopped
½ teaspoon salt
½ teaspoon dried parsley
½ teaspoon hot paprika
¼ teaspoon allspice
¼ teaspoon ground cardamom
2 medium acorn squash, halved and seeded

1. Preheat the oven to 350°F. In a skillet over low-medium heat, sauté all ingredients (except the squash), until evenly combined and aromatic. Spoon sautéed ingredients into the squash halves.

2. Place squash in an ungreased baking dish. Fill dish with hot water to a depth of ½". Cover and bake for 25 minutes.

3. Uncover and bake for another 20–25 minutes, until the squash is tender.

Harvest Spinach and Sprouts

The garlic and citrus that spice up the spinach and sprouts make this Harvest Spinach and Sprouts dish a bright, summery side dish! The Tabasco sauce used here provides a tart heat to the flavorful sautéed greens. Adding the sizzling hot Brussels sprouts to the bowl of spinach will help wilt the nutrient-dense leaves, shriveling them slightly while absorbing the zesty marinade.

1. In a large skillet, combine 2 tablespoons butter and 2 tablespoons canola oil. Heat over medium-high heat until butter has melted, then add 1 pound of Brussels sprouts and 1 clove of garlic to the melted butter. Cook and stir occasionally, until the Brussels sprouts soften and begin to brown, about 5–7 minutes. Spoon mixture over spinach in a large bowl.

2. Repeat process with remaining butter, oil, Brussels sprouts, and garlic. After about 5–6 minutes of cooking, add the red bell pepper and green onion, stirring well. Spoon it into the bowl over spinach.

3. Add lemon zest and juice, red pepper flakes, Tabasco, salt, and pepper, tossing gently. Serve warm.

Serves 8–10

4 tablespoons coconut butter, divided use

4 tablespoons canola oil, divided use

2 pounds Brussels sprouts, trimmed and sliced

2 cloves garlic, minced and divided

5 ounces baby spinach

1 red bell pepper, seeded and chopped

½ cup sliced green onion

1 tablespoon lemon zest

3 tablespoons lemon juice

1 tablespoon red pepper flakes

2 tablespoons Tabasco sauce

½ teaspoon salt

½ teaspoon ground black pepper

🌶 SPROUTED FROM BRUSSELS

Although Brussels sprouts are named after their Belgian origin, their roots trace back to an earlier date in history. Early forms of these cruciferous greens are said to have emerged from ancient Rome. Adverse to their smell? Don't overcook these baby cabbages, because doing so is the primary source of their unpleasant odor. Brussels sprouts are rich sources of vitamins A and C, folic acid, and dietary fiber.

Seasonably Seasoned Stuffing

This meaty, heavily spiced "stuffing" will truly be a crowd pleaser at your holiday get-together! The fresh herbs are a great way to merge all the flavors from each vegetable. Rosemary, thyme, and sage are great herbs to cook with turkey, and are accented by the spicy and peppery fennel and anise. Eliminate the ground turkey in this recipe to make it a vegetarian dish, and replace the meat with about 3–4 large heads of grated cauliflower!

Serves 12–14

1 teaspoon coconut oil
1 green bell pepper, chopped
2 (16-ounce) packages button mushrooms, chopped
1 cup celery, chopped
1 pound ground turkey (or pork)
1 onion, chopped
4–6 cloves garlic, minced
2 tablespoons rosemary, minced
2 tablespoons thyme, minced
2 tablespoons sage, minced
Salt and pepper, to taste
2 teaspoons fennel seeds
2 teaspoons anise
2 teaspoons paprika
½ teaspoon cayenne pepper

1. Preheat the oven to 325°F. Heat coconut oil in a large skillet on medium heat and sauté the green bell pepper, mushrooms, and celery.

2. In a large bowl, combine the ground turkey and all remaining ingredients. Add ground turkey mixture to skillet, and cook until turkey is browned slightly. Remove from heat and transfer to a baking dish. Bake uncovered 20–30 minutes, until the top of the stuffing is crispy.

🔥 HOW TO SAFELY PREPARE STUFFING

According to the USDA's Food Safety and Inspection Service, pre-cooking raw stuffing ingredients before stuffing your turkey helps reduce the risk of food-borne illness. Stuffing should be spooned into the bird loosely, and should be moist (not dry), because heat destroys bacteria more efficiently in a moist environment.

Buffalo Cauliflower

This Buffalo Cauliflower is a deliciously nutritious vegetarian take on the popular fried menu item: buffalo chicken bites. These will kick any spicy food craving and are very easy to make. And this recipe is not limited to cauliflower! You can replace it with other vegetables like broccoli, asparagus, zucchini, or summer squash for a bit of a deeper flavor. Try them all as a medley to really tantalize your taste buds! Try this hot and spicy recipe as a side dish or a simple snack.

1. Preheat the oven to 450°F. Mix together the almond flour, water, 1 teaspoon Tabasco or Frank's Red Hot sauce, and ½ teaspoon sea salt to form the batter. Dip the cauliflower in the batter until completely coated, and bake on a pre-greased baking sheet until batter hardens, about 15 minutes.

2. In a small bowl, mix ¼ cup of Tabasco or Hot Sauce, canola oil, and ½ teaspoon sea salt until combined. Brush the cooked cauliflower with sauce mixture until evenly coated, and bake again until crispy.

Serves 3

½ cup almond flour
½ cup water
1 teaspoon plus ¼ cup Tabasco or Frank's Red Hot sauce
1 teaspoon sea salt, divided use
1 head cauliflower (about 6 cups of florets)
¼ cup canola oil

Spicy Carrot Fries

Nothing is better than a sweet and spicy treat during dinner, and these Spicy Carrot Fries provide just that. Similar to a sweet potato fry, this recipe adds salt and spice to a sweet vegetable, and the results are phenomenal! These fries are a healthy, nutritious addition to any meal, and are satisfying to even the hardest-to-please palates. If you love the taste of this recipe but want to try something different, chop the carrots into chunks and coat them with the spicy marinade for a carrot-style home-fry recipe!

Serves 6

12 large carrots, peeled and cut into thick slices
1 tablespoon plus ¼ cup olive oil
2 cloves garlic, chopped
½ jalapeño, chopped
1 tablespoon lime juice
1 teaspoon cumin
1 teaspoon coriander
½ teaspoon crushed red pepper flakes
¼ teaspoon cayenne pepper
Dash salt and pepper

1. Preheat the oven to 400°F. Mix carrots with 1 tablespoon oil, and bake for 20 minutes.

2. Place all other ingredients (except for the ¼ cup olive oil) in a food processor or blender, and begin blending on low, while slowly adding the olive oil. Continue until evenly combined and smooth. Coat the cooked carrots with the seasoning mixture, tossing until evenly coated. Bake for an additional 5 minutes.

Sizzling Salsa-Topped Avocado Grillers

This recipe creates a creamy, charred snack or side dish with a ton of acidic punch! Upon grilling, the once-cool avocado becomes soft, warm, and smoky, and creates a delicious base for any topping. This spicy, tart tomato salsa is perfectly balanced by the avocado, and leaves your taste buds wanting more. This dish is perfect in spring or summer when avocados are at their freshest, and can be topped with any type of salsa or salad you happen to create!

1. Combine all ingredients (except avocados and 1 teaspoon oil) in a bowl and mix until evenly combined. Heat grill to high, brush avocado pieces lightly with reserved oil, and grill until lightly charred, about 1 minute each side.

2. Remove avocados from grill, and top each half with the sizzling salsa mixture.

Serves 4

1 large tomato, cored and cubed

1 tablespoon finely chopped green onion

1 tablespoon finely chopped dried thyme

1 tablespoon finely chopped cilantro

2 teaspoons finely chopped jalapeño (seeded)

1 teaspoon lime juice

½ teaspoon crushed red pepper flakes

⅛ teaspoon salt

2 avocados, halved, peeled, and pitted

2 teaspoons olive oil

Paleo-Style Seasoned "Breadsticks"

These breadsticks are a delicious Paleo version of a much sought-after dinner side, and they're also a great substitute for pizza crust! The fiery red pepper flakes give this "breadstick" its spice; however, it can be seasoned any way you like. Try using fresh chunks of roasted garlic, chopped jalapeño, or crushed peppercorns for added fiery flavor.

Yields 8 "breadsticks"

1 teaspoon olive oil
3 cups cauliflower florets, grated
1 egg, plus 1 egg white, lightly beaten
¼ cup coconut butter
1 tablespoon chopped cilantro
1 teaspoon dried basil
1 teaspoon oregano
1 teaspoon parsley
½ teaspoon crushed red pepper flakes

1. Preheat the oven to 350°F and grease a parchment-lined baking sheet with olive oil.

2. Mix all remaining ingredients in a bowl, until evenly combined. Spread the mixture evenly on the baking sheet, forming a large rectangle about ¾" thick.

3. Bake until lightly browned and slightly dried, about 40 minutes. Remove from oven, flip, and bake for an additional 8–10 minutes. Cut into 8–10 individual "breadsticks."

Spicy Sesame Eggplant

This versatile recipe tastes great with grilled meats, along with other roasted vegetables in a side dish, or chilled as a salad topper. It can also be used as a base for a burger dinner to replace the roll. The spicy chilies are what kick the spice up a notch and make this side even more intriguing. These flavorful eggplants also taste fantastic on the grill in the summer!

1. Preheat broiler. Place eggplant strips onto a baking sheet and toss with salt and pepper. Combine all remaining ingredients in a bowl, and mix well, forming a sauce.

2. Top eggplant slices evenly with sauce mixture, coating all slices equally. Broil the eggplant for about 15 minutes, or until browned and soft, stirring once or twice during cooking. Remove from heat and serve warm. These can also be served chilled as a salad topping, or as a cold side on a hot summer day.

Serves 3–4

2 medium eggplants (about 2 pounds), sliced and cut into ¾"-wide strips
2 teaspoons sea salt
¼ teaspoon ground pepper
2 tablespoons sesame seeds
2 tablespoons lime juice
1 tablespoon canola oil
1 tablespoon sesame oil
1 teaspoon fresh hot chilies
1 teaspoon finely minced garlic

Sautéed and Spicy Mushrooms

Mushrooms have a deep, meaty flavor, and the spicy paprika in this recipe gives them an added flair. They serve as a great side to many meals, but beautifully accent and create an added depth to beef dishes. This recipe is versatile, so feel free to choose what type of mushroom and spices you use! Shiitake mushrooms with a splash of coconut aminos and wasabi or portobello mushroom caps with Cajun seasoning are highly recommended.

Serves 2

2 tablespoons olive oil
2 tablespoons minced onion
2 tablespoons chopped celery
2 tablespoons minced garlic
2 cups button mushrooms
1–2 teaspoons hot paprika
½ teaspoon teaspoon cayenne pepper
3 tablespoons white wine
Salt and pepper, to taste

1. Heat olive oil over medium heat in a large frying pan. Add onion, celery, and garlic to the pan and sauté for 6–7 minutes. Add mushrooms, paprika, and cayenne pepper and cook for another 6–7 minutes.

2. Turm heat up to medium-high and let vegetables simmer for another minute. Add wine once the mushrooms start to smoke slightly. Let the wine evaporate and reduce. Sprinkle mushrooms with salt and pepper to taste and serve warm.

Spicy Carrot Hash

This impressive carrot recipe is so simple that it is certain to become an after-work staple on nights when you just don't feel like spending a ton of time in the kitchen. The cumin and ginger kick up the sweetness from the carrots and make for a tasty medley of flavors upon cooking. You can change up this recipe a bit by cutting the carrots into chunks and roasting with the spices instead. Once roasted, add them to a food processor to make a spiced carrot bisque!

1. Sauté the carrots and ginger in canola oil over medium-high heat until carrots dry out a bit and separate on their own, about 12–15 minutes.

2. Stir in remaining ingredients and serve immediately.

Serves 4

12 large carrots, shredded (about 4 cups)
2 tablespoons ground ginger
2 tablespoons canola oil
2½ tablespoons paprika
2½ tablespoons crushed red pepper flakes
3 teaspoons cumin seeds
Salt and pepper, to taste

Fiery Fried "Rice"

Grated/blended cauliflower is a staple for Paleo gurus looking to add that "rice" feel to meals! This rich, fried version is an amazing replacement for the typical dish you would find at any Asian-American style restaurant. The vegetables are flavorfully accented by the Asian-inspired tastes of Sriracha sauce and ginger. The egg adds protein to this dish, which helps make the leftovers a satisfying lunch option as well!

Serves 3–4

2 teaspoons coconut butter
½ yellow onion, finely diced
2 cloves garlic, minced
5 whole cremini mushrooms, thinly sliced
1 small red bell pepper, diced
1 small zucchini, diced
½ cup grated carrots
½ cup chopped green bell pepper
3 cups cauliflower florets, gently processed or blended to form the size and texture of rice
2 large eggs
5 tablespoons coconut aminos
2 teaspoons lemon juice
2 teaspoons ginger, minced
2 tablespoons chopped basil
1 tablespoon Sriracha sauce

1. Heat coconut butter in a large frying pan over medium heat. Add onions and garlic and sauté for about 5 minutes. Add the mushrooms and remaining vegetables and continue sautéing until tender. Stir in the "rice," cover, and cook for 5 minutes over low-medium heat.

2. Push all contents of the pan to one side, and scramble the 2 eggs on the other side of the pan. Combine the contents of both sides of the pan.

3. Combine the coconut aminos, lemon juice, and ginger in a small bowl and then add to the rice, along with the chopped basil and Sriracha, and cook for 1–2 more minutes. Serve warm.

Zesty Zucchini Chips

If you're looking for something that packs a whole lot of punch in each little chip, nothing beats these crispy, green Zesty Zucchini Chips! Slicing the zucchini with a mandoline makes perfectly even, thin slices that create a crunchier snack, and the lime juice and chili powder add spice and heat to the blank canvas of a plain zucchini. Once you pop one in your mouth, it will be impossible to stop!

1. Preheat the oven to 240°F. Combine the lime juice, chili powder, and lime zest, and mix until combined. Add zucchini slices and toss until evenly coated.

2. Place the zucchini slices on a parchment paper–lined baking sheet, sprinkle with salt, and drizzle with oil. Cook for 50–65 minutes, or until golden and crispy.

Serves 4

2 tablespoons lime juice
1 teaspoon chili powder
1 tablespoon lime zest
4 baby zucchini, sliced very thin
½ teaspoon salt
1 tablespoon canola oil

Spicy Sweet Potato Mash

This Spicy Sweet Potato Mash is an irresistible side dish that is perfect for the fall! There is a medley of flavors in this super simple dish, and they all blend together to create a sweet and spicy addition to any meal. This is a family favorite during Thanksgiving dinner, as the honey and spices mix so well with the sweet potato. If you'd like a whipped version of this recipe with fewer clumps, blend the roasted sweet potato in a food processor or with a handheld mixer.

Serves 4–6

4–5 large sweet potatoes, pierced and roasted until soft

2 tablespoons coconut butter

2 tablespoons raw organic honey

1 tablespoon chili powder

1 tablespoon cayenne pepper

1 teaspoon sea salt

1 teaspoon ground ginger

½ teaspoon black pepper

½ teaspoon cumin

1. Peel and cube the roasted sweet potatoes, place in a large bowl with coconut butter, and smash until fluffy.

2. Add the remaining ingredients, and stir until fully combined. Enjoy!

Sweet and Spicy Green Beans

Who knew that green beans made such a great side when honey and hot sauce are added? Well, now you know, and once you taste them, there's a good chance you'll become addicted! This Asian-inspired dish pairs nicely with steak or poultry, and is wonderful when enjoyed alongside (or in) the Fiery Fried "Rice" recipe found in this chapter. Add red pepper flakes to this recipe if you are looking for a bit more spice.

1. Add green beans to a medium sauce pot or steamer and add 1–2" water. Steam green beans for 3–5 minutes. Stir together the coconut aminos, garlic, honey, and hot sauce in a small bowl.

2. Add the steamed green beans to the canola oil in a large skillet and fry for 4–6 minutes over medium heat. Pour in the liquid mixture and continue stirring until most of the liquid has evaporated. Sprinkle with sesame seeds and serve warm.

Serves 2–4

12 ounces trimmed green beans
2 tablespoons coconut aminos
1 clove garlic, minced
1 teaspoon raw organic honey
½ teaspoon hot sauce (like Tabasco)
2 teaspoons canola oil
2 teaspoons sesame seeds

Racy Radish Potpourri

This Racy Radish Potpourri is an interesting way to eat radishes, and you won't want to stop! The habanero pepper used in this dish provides a *lot* of amazingly delicious heat, but if you're looking for a more mild spice, try using jalapeño or serrano peppers instead. This dish is great as a side or even as a salad topper to add a bit of flavor.

Serves 4

⅛ cup olive oil
⅛ cup coconut oil
1 tablespoon lemon juice
½ habanero pepper, chopped
2 (16-ounce) bags of radishes, cut into quarters
⅛ cup chives, chopped
1 tablespoon parsley, chopped
2 teaspoons capers, rinsed and drained

In a small bowl, combine the olive and coconut oil, lemon juice, and pepper to form the dressing. In a separate bowl, add radishes and all remaining ingredients, mix well, and add the dressing. Toss thoroughly and chill before serving.

Fiery Eggplant Fries

Who can resist a French fry—especially one that comes without the post-indulgence guilt? Try these delicious and nutritious fries and you won't be disappointed. Eggplant is such a versatile vegetable and can adapt to any spicy flavor it is coated in. In this dish, the chili powder, cumin, and cayenne pepper create a Mexican-style flavor and make these bite-size snacks simply irresistible! If you want these to be extra crispy, try placing them under the broiler for a few minutes after baking. Just be sure not to let them burn!

1. Preheat the oven to 400°F. Combine all spices and seasonings in a small bowl and mix well.

2. Place the eggplant pieces on baking sheet and drizzle with canola oil. Sprinkle seasoning mixture over eggplant, until evenly coated, leaving a small amount of the seasoning mix unused.

3. Bake eggplant until lightly browned and crispy, about 25 minutes. Remove from oven, and add remaining seasoning to the cooked "fries." Allow to cool slightly before serving.

Serves 3–4

1 teaspoon chili powder
1 teaspoon sea salt
1 teaspoon cumin
1 teaspoon cayenne pepper
1 teaspoon black pepper
2 medium eggplant, sliced into
   French fry–like strips
2 tablespoons canola oil

Grilled Broccolini

In this Grilled Broccolini dish, the bright, fresh notes of citrus play on your tongue while the chili flakes and cayenne heat your palate with each bite. The marinade and grilling techniques mentioned here can also be used with zucchini, asparagus, and other grill-worthy vegetables. And, as a grilled dish, this side pairs well with grilled meats and seafood. Add garlic and toasted pine nuts after grilling if you're looking for added flavor and texture.

Serves 3–4

2 pounds broccolini, cleaned and trimmed
Vegetable oil, as needed
Salt and pepper, to taste
2 tablespoons olive oil
2 tablespoons lemon juice
1 tablespoon lemon zest
1 teaspoon red chili flakes
½ teaspoon cayenne pepper

1. Toss cleaned broccolini with a small amount of vegetable oil and a sprinkle of salt and pepper. Coat grill grates with vegetable oil and grill over medium-high heat until lightly charred, about 6–8 minutes.

2. In a large bowl, combine olive oil, lemon juice, lemon zest, chili flakes, and cayenne pepper and mix well. Add the cooked broccolini and toss well until evenly coated. Serve immediately.

Savory Spiced Cabbage

This hot and spicy, Asian-style cabbage recipe can also be made with bok choy. Each option creates a light, earthy flavor with fiery spice. It accents chicken and shrimp dishes brilliantly. For added spice, top with a splash of Sriracha sauce before serving!

1. In a large skillet over medium heat, add canola oil. Cook green and red peppers, onion, and jalapeño until tender, about 8 minutes. Add tomatoes and honey and simmer for 3 minutes.

2. Add remaining ingredients and simmer another 15 minutes, stirring periodically. Serve warm.

Serves 3–4

1 teaspoon canola oil
½ cup chopped green bell pepper
½ cup chopped red bell pepper
½ cup chopped onion
1 teaspoon chopped jalapeño
1 (10-ounce) can tomatoes with green chilies, undrained, chopped
½ teaspoon raw organic honey
4 cups sliced cabbage
⅛ teaspoon black pepper
⅛ teaspoon hot pepper sauce

Blazing Bomba

This spicy condiment can be served as a topping on a homemade Paleo pizza, tossed amongst the veggies in a salad, served over a freshly cooked piece of fish or chicken, or alongside just about any entrée that could use a serious kick! This staple is the perfect "go-to" when guests stop by and you need a quick bite or last-minute appetizer. So keep a batch readily available in your refrigerator. When stored in an airtight container, this sultry snack will keep for at least a week.

Serves 3–4

1 large eggplant, diced
1 small fennel bulb, finely diced
¾ cup roasted red peppers, finely diced
1 large onion, finely diced
2–3 jalapeños, finely diced
½ cup green olives, drained, pitted, and finely diced
½ cup artichoke hearts, finely diced
2½ cups fresh cremini mushrooms, finely diced
3 large cloves garlic, minced
2 tablespoons olive oil
¼ teaspoon cayenne pepper
¼ teaspoon smoked paprika
2 tablespoons lime juice
Salt and freshly ground black pepper, to taste
½ cup parsley, chopped

1. In a large skillet, sauté all the vegetables (including garlic) in the olive oil until slightly softened, then add the cayenne and smoked paprika. Remove from heat and allow the cooked vegetables to cool on a baking sheet.

2. Transfer the vegetables to a bowl, and add the lime juice, salt and pepper to taste, and parsley.

3. Serve immediately, or store in an airtight container and refrigerate.

Spicy Cranberry Chutney

Not only is this delightful Spicy Cranberry Chutney tart and tasty, its warm flavor makes it a much desired side to just about any meal! This is a perfect holiday dish that complements turkey and sweet potatoes extremely well. The spice from the onion and jalapeño perfectly accent the light, fruity notes of the cranberries and the orange juice. Serve with dinner, as a salad topping, or as a spread for the Paleo-Style Seasoned "Breadsticks" found in this chapter!

Place all ingredients in a food processor or blender and blend until combined, but not completely smooth. Create a consistency that is slightly chunky. Chill overnight and serve.

Serves 6–8

4 cups cranberries
1½ jalapeños, chopped
⅓ red onion, chopped
1½ cups chopped cilantro
½ cup fresh orange juice
3 tablespoons raw organic
   honey
1 teaspoon sea salt

Jerk-Inspired Collard Greens

Collard greens are one of the most nutrient-dense foods available, and they aid your body in natural detoxification, fight illness, and help minimize inflammatory symptoms. You can't go wrong incorporating these wondrous greens into your next meal! This spicy, jerk-flavored version is pleasing to the palate and pairs well with a variety of different meals. Try adding fresh bacon bits as a topping for a little crunch and boost in flavor!

Serves 4–6

1 cup thinly sliced onion

1 red bell pepper, diced

2 tablespoons canola oil

½ habanero pepper, chopped

3 cloves garlic, minced

2 tablespoons dried thyme

2 tablespoons crushed red pepper flakes

6 cups collard greens, chopped

2 tablespoons coconut aminos

1 tomato, chopped

¼ teaspoon sea salt

¼ teaspoon black pepper

2 tablespoons lemon juice

1. Sauté onion and bell pepper in canola oil for 3–5 minutes in a large frying pan over medium heat, or until they begin to soften. Add habanero pepper, garlic, thyme, and crushed red pepper and continue sautéing for 2 minutes. Add the collard greens and coconut aminos, and stir.

2. Reduce heat to low, cover, and cook for 10 minutes. Stir in tomato, salt, and pepper, and cook until liquid begins to evaporate. Turn off heat and add lemon juice, stirring well, while removing collard greens from pan. Serve immediately.

Jerk-Spiced Brussels Sprouts

These super-flavorful Brussels sprouts are a great way to cook and serve a delicious and healthy vegetable. In this recipe, nutmeg blends nicely with the spice of the red pepper flakes, accenting the seared flavor of the Brussels sprouts. This dish also tastes great with bacon bits or prosciutto bites!

1. Bring water to a boil in a large pot and add Brussels sprouts and sea salt. Boil uncovered until slightly tender, about 5 minutes, and then drain.

2. Dry the pot, add the coconut oil, and sauté the garlic and red pepper flakes for 1 minute. Add Brussels sprouts and nutmeg and sauté for another 1–3 minutes, stirring occasionally. Remove from heat and serve warm.

Serves 2–4

2 quarts water
1 pound large Brussels sprouts, trimmed and quartered
1 teaspoon sea salt
2 tablespoons coconut oil
5 cloves garlic, minced
1 teaspoon red pepper flakes
½ teaspoon ground nutmeg

Stir-Fried Gingered Asparagus

This Stir-Fried Gingered Asparagus is best served alongside an Asian-inspired dinner because of its sweet and savory attributes. The zesty ginger and broth evenly coat every asparagus piece, creating one flavorful side dish. Add nuts like slivered almonds to this recipe for added crunch, add mushrooms for a deeper flavor, or add fresh lemon juice for its citrus notes. The choices are endless!

Serves 4

5–6 thin slices fresh ginger (sliced into coins)

2 tablespoons coconut oil

½ teaspoon sea salt

1 asparagus bunch, cut into pieces, separating stalks from tips

¼ cup low-sodium chicken broth

1 teaspoon sesame oil

1. Place ginger coins in coconut oil in a deep skillet over medium-high heat. Add salt and stir well to allow ginger to mix.

2. Add asparagus stalks to the pan, tossing well for 30 seconds–1 minute. Add asparagus tips to the pan and mix well. Add broth to pan, and continue stirring while cooking, until most of the broth has cooked down.

3. Add sesame oil to the pan, toss well, and remove from heat. Serve immediately.

Homemade Harissa

Harissa is a spicy, native African concoction that is super easy to make at home. Try this recipe and add to many dishes—including the Zesty Carrot Dip in Chapter 2 and the Sizzlin' Sweet Potato and Spinach Burrito in Chapter 4—for a kick! Your mouth will thank you.

Soak dried red chili peppers in water for about 30 minutes. When complete, remove stems and seeds. Add peppers with garlic, olive oil, cumin, coriander, cayenne pepper, and a pinch of salt and pepper to a blender. Blend to form a smooth paste. Store in the refrigerator for up to 1 month.

Yields about 1 cup

12 dried red chili peppers
1 cup water
2 cloves garlic
2 tablespoons olive oil
1 teaspoon cumin
1 teaspoon coriander
¼ teaspoon cayenne pepper
Pinch salt and pepper

Homemade Honey Mustard

Honey mustard is a delicious condiment for just about any food your heart desires, especially some freshly baked homemade pretzels! The spicy mustard and pepper provides an added kick to the sweet honey. Feel free to add a pinch of paprika and cayenne pepper to spice it up another notch!

Yields approximately 5 cups

1 egg
½ cup canola oil
½ teaspoon salt
½ teaspoon pepper
½ cup raw organic honey
¼ cup spicy mustard

Place egg, canola oil, salt, and pepper in bowl, and blend (with a hand blender) until creamy and thick. Stir in honey and mustard. This mixture keeps well in the refrigerator in an airtight container for up to 1 week.

🔥 MUSTARD MEMORABILIA MUSEUM!

Did you know there is a National Mustard Museum? First opened in 1992, the National Mustard Museum is located in Middleton, Wisconsin, and is home to the world's largest collection of mustards and mustard memorabilia, with more than 5,400 mustards from all 50 states and more than 70 countries. The National Mustard Museum even has its own recipe for mustard spice cake!

Paleo Mayo

Homemade, organic mayo is pretty simple to make. Once you try this at home, you will never resort to using store-bought mayonnaise again! You'll notice that this recipe isn't necessarily hot, but it takes on the flavors of spicy ingredients so easily that any fan of fiery food needs to have this Paleo Mayo in their arsenal. Make it often and don't be afraid to spice it up!

In a large glass bowl or container (preferably a Mason jar for easy storage after), blend all ingredients with an immersion blender, working your way up and down in the glass to make sure you reach every inch of the oil and the mayo becomes creamy and white. Store in a Mason jar or a glass, airtight container in the refrigerator for up to 1 month.

Yields 1 cup

1 large egg
1 cup extra-virgin olive oil
Juice of ½ lemon
¼ teaspoon salt

Cardamom-ized Carrot Pudding

Cardamom is the key ingredient in this sweetly spiced side dish, though it is also quite suitable as a dessert! This Indian-inspired dish utilizes the delightfully aromatic cardamom, a seasoning frequently used in Indian cooking. Honey is the sweetener here, but finely chopped pitted dates would be just as nice!

Serves 6

- 2 tablespoons coconut oil
- 6 medium carrots, peeled and grated
- 1 (14-ounce) can full-fat coconut milk
- 2 tablespoons raw organic honey
- 1 teaspoon ground cardamom
- ½ cup plus 2 tablespoons yellow raisins
- 2 tablespoons chopped pistachios, lightly toasted
- ⅓ cup Primal Whipped Cream, optional (see recipe in Chapter 7)

1. Melt the coconut oil in a medium saucepan over medium heat, and then add the grated carrots. Cook for about 10 minutes, stirring periodically, until carrots have begun to soften. Add the coconut milk, honey, and ground cardamom, and stir well to combine. Bring the mixture to a boil, then reduce the heat to a low boil. Boil for about 20 minutes, stirring often, until the carrots are very soft. Stir in ¼ cup of the yellow raisins.

2. Place the mixture in a blender or food processor, and blend briefly so that the mixture is smooth but specks of carrot and raisins are still visible.

3. Transfer pudding to 6 individual ramekins and top each with a bit of raisins, pistachios, and dollop of Primal Whipped Cream, if desired (especially if serving as dessert). Best when served warm.

CHAPTER 6
Snacks

Hunger can strike at any time, even sometimes when you least expect it. From longtime primal eating extremists to Paleo "newbies," everyone needs a snack from time to time. Devising some Paleo-friendly treats is critical to successfully adhering to the lifestyle's multiple dietary restrictions, especially since all those quick, easily obtained convenience foods are rarely Paleo-approved. The recipes you'll find in this chapter—from Coconut Crisps to Cracked Pepper Crackers to Blistering Beef Jerky—have a variety of hot and spicy flavors and are guaranteed to fill you up with the foods you want and the flavors you crave. These fiery creations are packed with a diverse array of peppery, savory, and aromatic ingredients, yielding snacks that are nothing short of irresistible.

Slow-Cooked Spicy Salsa

Enjoy this salsa as a spicy, nutritious, low-calorie dip, as a marinade, or as a complementary side to your favorite Southwest-inspired dish! Cooking these ingredients in a slow cooker allows the tomatoes and jalapeños to soften and provide acidity, so the vegetables can break down and the flavors can meld together. Try increasing the heat by adding half of a habanero pepper, or sweeten it up a bit with some mango or pineapple chunks.

Serves 16

10 fresh Roma or plum tomatoes, chopped
2 cloves garlic, minced
1 large onion, chopped
2 jalapeño peppers, stems removed and chopped (remove seeds for milder salsa)
1 large green bell pepper, chopped
¼ cup fresh cilantro leaves
½ teaspoon lemon juice

1. Place chopped tomatoes, minced garlic, and chopped onions in a 3–4-quart slow cooker and stir to combine.

2. Stir jalapeño peppers and bell peppers into the slow cooker. Cover and cook on high for 2½–3 hours.

3. When cool, combine mixture with cilantro leaves and lemon juice and blend in a food processor until desired consistency is reached.

Slow-Cooked Almonds with a Kick

These crunchy, heart-healthy snacks are hard to resist. They are a simple, one-pot creation that can be enjoyed as a cocktail snack or an after-gym, nutrient-packed pick-me-up. And if you're tired of snacking on the same old thing, don't worry! This recipe gives you the ability to tap into your creative side. Add more spice with some cayenne pepper, or some ginger and cumin for a more Middle-Eastern inspired snack.

1. Heat a 4-quart slow cooker on high for 15 minutes. Add the almonds. Drizzle oil over almonds and stir. Sprinkle with garlic and pepper, and stir.

2. Cover and cook on low for 2 hours. Stir every 30 minutes.

3. Turn heat up to high, and cook uncovered for 30 minutes, stirring every 15 minutes.

4. Turn heat to low and serve warm, or remove from heat and allow to cool.

Serves 24

6 cups whole, unblanched almonds
4 tablespoons coconut oil
3 cloves garlic, minced
2–3 teaspoons coarsely ground pepper

Hot Cinnamon Chili Walnuts

How could these Hot Cinnamon Chili Walnuts not be a hit with the chili powder, cinnamon, and honey medley? This is a sweet, sultry, and spicy way to eat walnuts, and they're a great addition to any side dish. Try adding these walnuts to the Sweet and Spicy Green Beans or Stir-Fried Gingered Asparagus in Chapter 5. Or, try this dish as a flavorful snack in between meals.

Serves 6

1½ cups walnuts
¼ cup raw organic honey
2 teaspoons cinnamon
1½ teaspoons chili powder
2 teaspoons coconut oil

1. Combine all the ingredients and place in a greased 2½-quart slow cooker. Cover slow cooker and vent lid with a chopstick or the handle of a wooden spoon. Cook on high for 2 hours or on low for 4 hours. If using a larger slow cooker, you will probably need to reduce the cooking time to only 1 hour on high, or 2 hours on low.

2. Pour walnut mixture out onto a baking sheet lined with parchment paper. Allow to cool and dry, and then transfer to a container with an airtight lid. Store in the pantry for up to 2 weeks.

Hot Chicken Buffalo Bites

Love buffalo wings? Then you will love these Hot Chicken Buffalo Bites even more! They are super easy, much less messy, and are made with juicy chicken breasts so you won't have to worry about any bones. The almond flour coating used here serves as a "dredge" in this recipe, and helps the hot sauce adhere to every inch of the chicken breast strips. This is a great appetizer or small meal, and goes well with sticks of celery and carrots, which help cool the palate.

1. Place chicken pieces into a greased 2½-quart slow cooker.

2. In a saucepan, whisk together the almond flour and melted coconut butter for 2–3 minutes to toast the flour. Slowly whisk in the garlic and Frank's Red Hot sauce. Pour sauce over chicken in the slow cooker.

3. Cover and cook on high for 3 hours or on low for 6 hours. (If using a larger slow cooker, make sure to reduce cooking time by about half.) Serve with celery and carrot sticks.

Serves 6

3 large chicken breasts, cut into 2" strips
2 tablespoons almond flour
¼ cup melted coconut butter
3 cloves garlic, peeled and minced
⅓ cup Frank's Red Hot sauce

🔥 FRESH GARLIC VERSUS GARLIC POWDER

In a pinch you can use 1½ teaspoons garlic powder in this recipe. The garlic flavor won't be quite as pungent and rich as it would if you used fresh garlic, but the dish will still be easy and enjoyable. If you do use fresh garlic, be sure to keep in a location with good air circulation. Do not store fresh garlic bulbs in plastic bags or sealed containers, as this can cause mold. Store the bulbs in a well-ventilated area, like a mesh or wire basket, to allow the garlic to breathe, and help extend its shelf life.

Sweet and Spicy Pecans

These Sweet and Spicy Pecans are super addictive. This recipe makes a crunchy, sticky snack that is so hard to stop eating, and even harder to share! A perfect balance of spicy and sweet, the honey and ginger harmonize beautifully with their zesty counterparts: paprika, cayenne, and black pepper. You may want to double or triple this recipe, since you'll quickly be back for more! These keep for up to 1 week when stored in an airtight container.

Yields 4 cups

4 cups pecans
½ cup raw organic honey
2 tablespoons coconut butter, melted
½ teaspoon sea salt
½ teaspoon ginger
½ teaspoon cayenne pepper
¼ teaspoon freshly ground black pepper
¼ teaspoon paprika
1 large egg white, at room temperature

1. Preheat the oven to 350°F. Spread the pecans on a baking sheet and toast for about 10 minutes. Let the pecans cool and lower the oven temperature to 250°F.

2. Line 2 baking sheets with parchment paper. In a large bowl, toss the pecans with the honey, coconut butter, salt, ginger, cayenne pepper, black pepper, and paprika.

3. In a separate bowl, whisk the egg white until frothy. Add the egg white to the pecans and toss well.

4. Spread the pecans on the baking sheets in a single layer. Bake for about 20–30 minutes, or until the nuts are golden brown, being careful not to burn. Once golden brown, immediately loosen the pecans from the parchment paper with a spatula, and let cool completely on the baking sheets before serving.

Spicy Pumpkin Seeds

Make a double batch of these Spicy Pumpkin Seeds, because this crispy, savory snack will be gobbled up in no time! The mouthwatering mix of spices and flavors will keep you coming back for more. There is a lot of room for variation here as well. A blend of Tabasco, cayenne, cumin, and chili powder is delicious, but go ahead and feel free to mix and match. Try a little paprika, sea salt, or your own chipotle spice creation!

1. Preheat the oven to 300°F and place the pumpkin seeds on an ungreased baking sheet.

2. Mix the butter (or ghee) and Tabasco sauce, and pour it over the seeds.

3. Combine all the spices and sprinkle over the freshly coated pumpkin seeds. Toss well until evenly coated.

4. Bake for 30–40 minutes, or until golden and crispy, stirring the seeds halfway through. Store in an airtight container.

Yields 2 cups

2 cups pumpkin seeds
¼ cup clarified butter or ghee, melted
½ teaspoon Tabasco sauce
1 teaspoon cayenne pepper
½ teaspoon cumin
1 tablespoon chili powder

Coconut Crisps

These crunchy chips are simply crazy good. They are sweet, salty, and spiced just right! They're everything you'd want in a snack, all in one recipe. Consider doubling or tripling up on these amounts, because one batch won't last! The sugary flavor from the sweet components—coconut sugar, cinnamon, and coconut chips—is extraordinary when paired with their sultry counterparts, the coriander, cardamom, and ginger. These Coconut Crisps are guaranteed to meet all your taste buds' needs!

Yields 3 cups

1 cup coconut milk

¼ cup coconut sugar

½ teaspoon sea salt

½ teaspoon cinnamon

½ teaspoon ginger

½ teaspoon cardamom

¼ teaspoon ground coriander

3 cups coconut chips (ribbon coconut), soaked in water for 1–2 hours

1. In a large bowl, combine all ingredients, adding the coconut chips last.

2. Preheat the oven to 200°F. Spread soaked chips in a thin layer on a parchment-lined baking sheet and bake for 2 hours.

3. Remove the coconut chips from the oven and increase the heat to 400°F. Return chips to the oven, and cook for 10–20 minutes or until they are golden and crispy. Be careful not to burn. Allow to cool before serving.

🌶 SPOTLIGHT ON COCONUT SUGAR

Coconut sugar, also called coconut palm sugar, is derived from the sap of the coconut plant. Once obtained from the flowers of the coconut palm, the sap is placed under heat to allow the water to evaporate. The end product is coconut sugar. Although it contains nutrients like iron, zinc, calcium, and potassium, you'd have to consume quite a bit in order to acquire modest amounts of these minerals. In addition, coconut sugar is very high in calories, so as with regular sugar, use it sparingly!

Cinnamon-Ginger-Almond Butter

An exciting, flavorful twist on nut butter, this Cinnamon-Ginger-Almond Butter is out of this world! The natural sweetness from the honey and almonds is highlighted nicely by cinnamon and sea salt. In addition, the hot and spicy ginger and cardamom give this dish just the right amount of edge. Exuberantly fulfilling, you'll never want to see an empty jar!

1. Combine all ingredients in a food processor, and allow to fully process (about 15–20 minutes).

2. Transfer to a sealed glass jar and consume within 2 weeks, or store it in the fridge for up to 1 month.

Yields 1½ cups

3 cups raw organic almonds
1½ ounces raw organic honey
½ teaspoon sea salt
1 teaspoon cinnamon
1 teaspoon ginger
1 teaspoon cardamom

Curried Coconut Pretzel Sticks

Commercially prepared pretzels are Paleo prohibited. This version how-ever, doesn't use any Paleo-banned grains or flour and makes thicker, softer pretzels that pair marvelously with some Homemade Honey Mustard (see Chapter 5). For all you salty pretzel lovers, use some of the egg for an egg wash during the final few minutes of baking (you'll want to cut and form your pretzels first), and sprinkle some coarse salt over the nearly cooked dough. Craving some more crunch? Use one less egg, and only 1 table-spoon of coconut butter. Once your dough is cooked, cut into small narrow "sticks." Enjoy these spectacular hot and spicy sticks.

Yields about 2 cups of "pretzel dough"

3 eggs
1½ cups almond flour
2 tablespoons coconut butter
3 tablespoons coconut flour
1 tablespoon curry powder
2 teaspoons salt
½ teaspoon turmeric
½ teaspoon cumin
1 batch Homemade Honey Mustard (see Chapter 5)

1. Preheat the oven to 350°F. Place all the ingredients into a bowl and mix well until a dough is formed.

2. Let the dough sit for 5 minutes or more, and then roll it into pretzel sticks (forming any shape your creativity concocts), and place them on a parchment paper–lined cookie sheet.

3. Bake the pretzels for 8–10 minutes, and remove from heat. Turn the oven up to 400°F, flip the pretzels, and return the cookie sheet to the oven for about 5 more minutes, until the pretzels start to brown.

4. Allow to cool, or serve warm with Home-made Honey Mustard dipping sauce (see Chapter 5).

Spicy Sweet Potato Chips

These chips are a fabulous, mouthwatering, sweet and spicy, crunchy treat. Impossible to eat just one, they will forever change the way you look at chips. The fiery mix of paprika and chili pepper mixes with the natural sugars of the sweet potatoes, and really turns the heat up on flavor! Canola or olive oil would also suffice for the coconut oil here, and can be applied by tossing the uncooked chips in a bowl of oil, or by shaking inside a sealed plastic bag until evenly coated.

1. Preheat the oven to 275°F. Evenly brush all sides of each potato slice with coconut oil.

2. Place chips in a single layer on 1–2 parchment paper–lined baking sheets. Bake for about 40 minutes, and be careful not to burn or brown too darkly.

3. Remove the chips from the oven, and turn them upside down to expose the more oily side, and sprinkle with half of the salt, chili pepper, and paprika.

4. Remove chips from the pan and flip them over, placing them upside down on a plate. Add the remainder of the salt, pepper, and paprika, the same way you did the first time around. Serve warm or cooled; they are just as tasty either way!

Yields 3–4 cups

1 sweet potato, thinly sliced
2 tablespoons coconut oil, melted
1 teaspoon sea salt
1 teaspoon chipotle chili pepper
1 teaspoon smoked paprika

THE SENSATIONAL SWEET POTATO

Sweet potatoes are one of the most nutritionally valuable root vegetables. These orange-hued tubers are rich sources of vital nutrients like vitamin C, calcium, folate, potassium, and beta-carotene. They are super easy to grow even for novice gardeners, requiring only 100 days without frost, so you don't have to reside in the tropics to make these nutritious tubers part of next season's harvest!

Savory Seaweed Strips

Nori seaweed, or algae, has been a staple in Japanese cuisine dating back to the eighth century. Nori sheets are crunchy, dried, and paper-thin from the low temperature drying process. These salty sheets of seaweed are most often used in rolls of sushi. This recipe kicks the flavor up a notch with the incorporation of cayenne and black pepper, creating a savory yet spicy snack!

Yields 42 chips

12 nori sheets
¼ cup water
3 cloves garlic, minced
1 tablespoon olive oil
1 teaspoon ground cayenne pepper
½ teaspoon black pepper
Salt, to taste
2–3 teaspoons sesame seeds

1. Preheat the oven to 275°F and cover two large baking sheets with aluminum foil. Place 6 sheets of nori in a single layer on the baking sheets, shiny side up, and lightly brush the nori with water from edge to edge.

2. Next, align another sheet of nori on top of each of the 6 previously placed sheets and press the two together.

3. Using a sharp knife, cut the nori into 1" strips lengthwise, then cut those strips in half, horizontally, resulting in 42 chips. Arrange the chips in a single layer on the baking sheets.

4. Combine the garlic, olive oil, cayenne, and black pepper in a small bowl. Lightly brush the chips with more water, followed by the garlic, olive oil, and pepper mixture, and then sprinkle generously with salt, followed by the sesame seeds.

5. Place the baking sheet on the middle rack of the oven, and bake for 15–20 minutes, or until they turn to a deep green color. Remove from the oven and sprinkle with more salt if desired. Allow to cool before eating for optimal crunch!

Apples Ablaze

This dish gives you a spiced-up, exciting new way to eat your applesauce! Using clarified butter creates a rich, smooth, and decadent dish, perfect for use as a succulent side to the main course, or as an absolutely divine dessert. Enjoyed hot or cold, this sweet and spicy recipe is loaded with vitamin C, fiber, and a combination of cinnamon, ginger, cloves, and nutmeg—a foursome that never fails to please!

1. Combine apples, water, and lemon juice in a large saucepan, bring to a boil, and then turn down the heat. Cover and simmer for 25 minutes or until apples are tender.

2. Stir in the cherries, apricots, cinnamon, ginger, cloves, and nutmeg, and cook 5 more minutes.

3. Add the clarified butter to the hot mixture and stir until melted. Garnish with lemon zest.

Serves 6–8

6 apples, peeled, cored, and sliced (Gala apples are recommended)

1 cup water

2 tablespoons lemon juice

2 tablespoons chopped unsweetened dried cherries

½ cup chopped dried apricots

2 teaspoons cinnamon

¼ teaspoon ginger

¼ teaspoon ground cloves

¼ teaspoon nutmeg

2 tablespoons clarified butter

1 tablespoon fresh lemon zest, for garnish

🔥 BAKING WITH APPLES

Gala apples have a mildly sweet flavor and are the best choice for salads, applesauce, and eating fresh. Sour and crisp Granny Smith are an all-purpose cooking apple, and one of the most popular tart apples. McIntosh are perfect for eating fresh, though their flavor tends to break down when heated. Cortland apples are excellent baking apples; their resilient hue makes them a popular choice for pies and crisps.

Peppery Prosciutto Chips

These Paleo crisps are instantaneously mouthwatering due to a knock-your-socks-off combination of salty, savory, spicy, and super crunchy. These chips turn up the heat with a trio of black, cayenne, and red pepper, but they don't stop there! These are even tasty just plain, so any spices you choose will only enhance their hot and spicy potential.

Serves 2–4

½ teaspoon finely crushed black pepper
½ teaspoon finely crushed cayenne pepper
½ teaspoon finely crushed red pepper
6 ounces fresh prosciutto, thinly sliced

1. Preheat the oven to 350°F. Combine spices in a small bowl.

2. Line 1–2 cookie sheets with parchment paper. Place the prosciutto slices in a single layer on the sheet(s). Sprinkle evenly with spices.

3. Place the sheet(s) in the oven on the middle rack, and bake for 10–15 minutes or until crunchy. Remove from heat and transfer the chips to a cooling rack, which allows them to become even crunchier.

Blistering Beef Jerky

You will not be able to resist this tasty, convenient, protein-packed snack! You've seen beef jerky in stores, but this spicy, fulfilling treat is much healthier when homemade. It contains none of the additives or nitrates often found in the commercially produced versions. This dish packs in a ton of heat from the very first bite, but can be altered depending on how daring your taste buds are. Add more cayenne and red pepper flakes if you like it *hot*.

1. In a medium stock pot, combine coconut aminos, Worcestershire sauce, water, liquid smoke, and all spices (except the red pepper flakes). Heat over low heat until it is warmed through.

2. While sauces and spices are heating, use a mandoline (or knife) to slice your beef into thin ¼" slices. Make sure the beef is cold for easier slicing. Set aside.

3. Pour marinade into a large storage container with a lid. Once cooled slightly, add sliced beef to the container, making sure each piece is coated in marinade. Place in refrigerator overnight, shaking container occasionally.

4. After the beef and marinade has had time to set overnight, place beef in a colander and quickly rinse with water. Set your dehydrator to 160–170°F, and lay beef in a single layer on the shelves of your dehydrator (do not overlap slices). Dehydrate for approximately 4–4½ hours, or until the edges of the beef start to crack slightly. Set aside and let cool.

5. Coat slices with red pepper flakes for added spice. Store in the refrigerator for about 30 days in a sealed, airtight container.

Yields 2 pounds jerky

½ cup coconut aminos
½ cup Worcestershire sauce
½ cup water
½ tablespoon liquid smoke
1 tablespoon garlic powder
½ tablespoon paprika
½ tablespoon chili powder
1 teaspoon black pepper
½ teaspoon cayenne pepper
2 pounds London broil
2 tablespoons red pepper flakes

Bold Baba Ghanouj

This super-spicy version of baba ghanouj, a beloved Middle-Eastern dip, is a taste bud pleaser! The eggplant really absorbs the hot flavors of all the spices and serves as delicious base for a dip. This spread is a perfect accompaniment to fresh cut vegetables or as a side dipping sauce to your favorite main course. Double this batch and bring it as an appetizer to your next dinner party!

Yields 1–1½ cups

1 large eggplant, peeled and chopped
3 cloves garlic, peeled
4 tablespoons olive oil, divided use
Salt and pepper, to taste
¼ cup tahini
Juice of 1 lemon
1 teaspoon cayenne pepper
½ teaspoon paprika
½ teaspoon cumin
Chopped parsley, for garnish

1. Preheat the oven to 400°F. Coat the eggplant chunks and garlic with 1 tablespoon olive oil, and sprinkle with salt and pepper. Place on a foil-lined baking sheet and roast for 30 minutes, tossing occasionally, until browned and soft. Remove from heat and allow to cool.

2. Add eggplant, garlic, and all other ingredients (except for the remaining olive oil) to a food processor. Blend and slowly incorporate olive oil until a smooth consistency is reached.

3. Chill in the refrigerator until ready to serve. Top with freshly cut parsley. Perfect with the Cracked Pepper Crackers, found in this chapter.

Cracked Pepper Crackers

Traditional, white flour and grain-based crackers are not Paleo-approved, but these almond flour–based goodies are a delightful replacement. These crunchy snacks are super peppery, and they're a perfect option to serve with pepperoni or a delicious dip, like the Bold Baba Ghanouj (see recipe in this chapter). The crushed red peppers and rosemary team up with the black pepper to create a fiery flavor and real mouthwatering crackers filled with crunch!

1. Preheat the oven to 350°F. Combine almond flour, black pepper, red pepper flakes, rosemary, and salt in a large mixing bowl. In a separate small mixing bowl, whisk together the egg, olive oil, water, and honey until frothy. Add wet ingredients to dry ingredients bowl, and stir until well blended.

2. Place dough between 2 sheets of parchment paper, and use a rolling pin to roll into a thin sheet, approximately ⅛" thick. Remove top layer of parchment paper. With a pizza cutter, cut away extra dough to make a perfect square. With a marinade brush, coat the top of the dough with the melted clarified butter. Cut dough into small 1½" squares.

3. Place the dough (still on top of the parchment paper) into the oven and bake for about 10 minutes, until tops start to turn a light golden color. Remove from oven and let cool before serving.

Yields approximately 20 crackers

2½ cups almond flour
2 tablespoons coarsely ground black pepper
1 tablespoon red pepper flakes, finely ground (a mortar and pestle work well for this process)
1 teaspoon dried rosemary, finely chopped
1 teaspoon salt
1 egg
1 tablespoon olive oil
1 tablespoon water
1 teaspoon raw organic honey
1 tablespoon clarified butter, melted

Tasty Trail Mix

This sweet and spicy nut mixture is a great snack to take with you for a day of hiking or as a grab-and-go snack after working out. The stickiness from the maple syrup allows the zesty spices to adhere nicely to each nut, providing tons of flavor within each handful. Vary this recipe by using a variety of different nutty combinations. Consider using macadamia nuts, pumpkin seeds, and walnuts, but don't stop there. The sky's the limit with this Tasty Trail Mix!

Yields 2 cups

2 cups of a nut medley (try using unsalted almonds, cashews, and sunflower seeds)
1½ tablespoons pure maple syrup
1½ tablespoons coconut oil, melted
½ teaspoon cinnamon
½ teaspoon cardamom
½ teaspoon chili powder
¼ teaspoon cayenne pepper
Pinch salt

1. Preheat the oven to 350°F. Place nuts on a parchment paper–lined baking sheet. Roast for 5–7 minutes.

2. While nuts are roasting, combine the rest of the ingredients in a large bowl and whisk together until well blended. Remove nuts from oven and let cool slightly. Add nuts to maple syrup mixture and stir so all nuts are coated.

3. Return nuts to the baking sheet and place back in the oven for an additional 5–10 minutes. Watch to make sure the nuts do not burn with the maple syrup mixture on them.

4. Remove from oven and allow to cool completely. Break up the nuts and serve!

Fiery Fried Figs

These sweet and fiery pan-fried figs are an addictive treat that is so easy to pop in your mouth! Figs are valuable ingredients in any dish; they are high in fiber and potassium and can curb sugar cravings with their rich, sweet flavor. In this recipe, the sweet fig and honey blend deliciously with the sultriness of the Sriracha, as well as with the kick from the cinnamon and ginger combination. In addition to being a perfect snack, this recipe works well as a salad topping or dessert.

Yields 16 fig bites

1 tablespoon coconut oil
1 tablespoon raw organic honey
1 tablespoon Sriracha sauce
½ teaspoon cinnamon
½ teaspoon ground ginger
8 fresh figs, halved
1 batch Sweet and Spicy Dipping Sauce (see recipe in this chapter)

1. In a medium skillet, melt the coconut oil over medium heat. Add honey, Sriracha, cinnamon, and ginger and mix with a wooden spoon until well blended. Let mixture sit on heat until it starts to simmer. Turn heat to medium-high heat if necessary, but be cautious of the honey burning.

2. Place fig halves, flesh side down, into bubbling honey mixture, moving them around in the pan occasionally. Let them pan fry for about 5–7 minutes, or until figs start to brown and caramelize.

3. Serve this snack warm with or without Sweet and Spicy Dipping Sauce.

Sweet and Spicy Dipping Sauce

This Sweet and Spicy Dipping Sauce is absolutely delicious when served with Fiery Fried Figs (see recipe in this chapter). This creamy sauce works hard to accent the fiery flavors in that honey mixture and is guaranteed to brighten up your day! Enjoy this creamy topping as a sweet and wonderfully flavorful addition to your favorite dessert!

Yields 1 cup

1 cup unsweetened coconut yogurt
2 tablespoons raw organic honey
1 teaspoon vanilla extract
1 teaspoon cinnamon
½ teaspoon nutmeg

Stir together all ingredients for a sweet and velvety dipping sauce. Store in an airtight container in the refrigerator for up to 1 week.

🔥 FUN FIG FACTS!

Multiple tiny flowers produce the crunchy little edible seeds that give figs their unique texture. Figs help naturally hold in the moisture in baked goods, helping them stay fresher, and fig purée is often used to replace fat in baked goods. The first commercial product appearance of this amazing fruit was made with the introduction of Fig Newtons in 1891!

Ferocious Fried Green Tomatoes

This traditional Southern dish is a real tangy treat, but it can also be enjoyed as a side to an entrée of your choice. Experiment with different spices to blend into the flour, a technique known as breading, and make this dish even hotter—if you can stand it! The Tabasco drizzle that tops these Ferocious Fried Green Tomatoes really pulls out the spice in this recipe. You'll crave a second helping!

Yields 12–15 tomato slices

1 cup almond flour
1 teaspoon cayenne pepper
1 teaspoon paprika
1 teaspoon garlic powder
Pinch salt and pepper
2 eggs
1 teaspoon water
3 large, firm green tomatoes, husks removed, cut into ¼"-thick slices
Drizzle of olive oil
Tabasco sauce, for garnish

1. Set oven to broil on high and place oven rack no more than 6" away from the top of the oven. Combine almond flour, cayenne pepper, paprika, garlic powder, salt, and pepper in a flat, shallow bowl and stir.

2. Combine the eggs and water in a separate shallow bowl and whisk until blended and frothy.

3. Dip each slice of tomato into the egg mixture, and then into the almond flour to coat. Place the tomato slices on a lightly oiled baking sheet, making sure not to overlap. Drizzle a small amount of olive oil over each tomato. Broil, in batches if necessary, for about 6 minutes, and then flip. Broil for another 6 minutes and remove. Serve hot with a drizzle of Tabasco sauce on top.

Cardamom Cooler

This cool and creamy smoothie-like cooler is a sweet and punchy treat on a hot day. The pungent ground cardamom and spicy ginger use their heat to accent the sweetness from the vanilla and banana. To switch things up a bit, try this recipe warm! Just omit the ice, and once the mixture is puréed, place it back on the heat to simmer. Add a touch of cacao, or even some coffee for a deliciously warming drink—in both temperature and taste!

Serves 2

2 cups coconut milk
¼ cup unsweetened coconut milk creamer
1 overripe banana, sliced
2 tablespoons raw organic honey
1 teaspoon vanilla extract
1 teaspoon ground cardamom
1 teaspoon cinnamon plus extra for garnish
½ teaspoon ground ginger
2 cups ice

1. Pour all ingredients (except the ice) into a medium sauce pot. Turn heat to medium and bring mixture to a low simmer. Let simmer on low for about 5 minutes, stirring frequently. Remove from heat to cool.

2. Once cooled, pour mixture into blender and purée until you reach a smooth consistency. Add ice to the creamy mixture for added crunch and smoothie-like consistency. Serve cold, and sprinkle top with extra cinnamon.

Portobello Cap Personal Pizzas

There is nothing better than a deliciously roasted portobello mushroom cap filled with spicy sauce, hearty meat, and sautéed vegetables! These Portobello Cap Personal Pizzas are both healthy *and* satisfying and taste great as a snack, side dish, or for lunch! There are many ways to add some extra spice to this recipe if you're looking for more heat. Just marinate the portobello mushroom in herbs and spices before adding toppings, or add jalapeños and other peppers as the vegetable topping. A dish this flexible helps add variety to your everyday meals!

1. Preheat the oven to 350°F. Line a baking sheet with parchment paper or foil and place 4 mushroom caps, top side down, on the sheet.

2. Heat ground beef over medium-high heat in a medium skillet until cooked through but still juicy. Drain fats and add cayenne pepper and red pepper flakes. Stir together until well blended. Add a quarter of the meat to each portobello mushroom cap. Top each meat-filled mushroom with desired amount of spicy marinara sauce (½ cup recommended), chopped onions, and peppers. Top off each with a small drizzle of olive oil and salt and pepper to taste.

3. Bake in the oven for about 20–25 minutes, until mushrooms and vegetable toppings are well roasted. Remove from heat and enjoy hot.

Serves 4

4 large portobello mushroom caps
½ pound lean ground beef
½ teaspoon cayenne pepper
¼ teaspoon red pepper flakes
2 cups Fiery Marinara (see recipe for Bison Meatballs and Fiery Marinara in Chapter 2)
½ cup chopped onions
½ cup chopped bell peppers
Drizzle of olive oil
Salt and pepper, to taste

🔥 MUSHROOM MADNESS

Using portobello mushroom caps is a wonderful way to present food. They are large, resilient, and have an earthy, meaty flavor that adds depth to many meals. Try filling your roasted portobello mushroom cap with a breakfast dish like the Tasty Taco Scramble (see Chapter 1) or fill them with cauliflower couscous or "rice" for a superbly satisfying side.

Wild Wasabi Nuts

These spicy, wasabi-coated nuts are finger-licking good! The pungent spice from the wasabi takes the lead role in this dish and adds an amazing, Asian-inspired flavor to this high-protein snack. These nuts store well, and are a great quick treat. Make a double batch for your next party because they're guaranteed to disappear fast!

Serves 8–10

1 egg white
1 tablespoon coconut aminos
½ pound raw almonds
½ pound macadamia nuts
2 teaspoons coconut flour
2½ tablespoons wasabi powder, plus more if desired
1½ teaspoons sea salt
Drizzle of olive oil

1. Preheat the oven to 275°F. Line a baking sheet with lightly oiled parchment paper.

2. Whisk egg white and coconut aminos until frothy in a medium bowl. Add nuts and stir so all are coated. Combine coconut flour, wasabi powder, and sea salt in a large sealable plastic bag, and shake. Add the nuts to the bag and shake until they are all well coated. Add more wasabi powder here if additional spiciness is desired.

3. Pour the nuts onto lined baking sheet and toss so they are in a single layer. Bake for about 15 minutes, then turn off the heat, but let the nuts sit in the oven for another 10 minutes to continue roasting slowly. Cool, drizzle with olive oil, and serve.

Kickin' Kale Chips

A great way to incorporate kale into your diet—crunchy and covered in a salty spice—these crunchy little snack bites are outrageously delicious! One bite and you will be hooked. Believe it or not, these Kickin' Kale Chips are an addictive replacement to potato chips for those living the Paleo lifestyle! Lighter, and obviously green, the nutrient content in this recipe surpasses any other kind of "chip" you've ever had!

1. Preheat the oven to 300°F. Mix all ingredients in a large bowl until evenly coated.

2. Place kale on baking sheets in a single layer. Bake until crispy, about 20 minutes, flipping halfway through. Remove from heat and allow to cool before serving.

Serves 2–4

Leaves from 1 large bunch of kale, torn into large pieces and patted dry
3 tablespoons canola oil
½ teaspoon Tabasco sauce
½ teaspoon cayenne pepper
¼ teaspoon sea salt
¼ teaspoon chili powder
¼ teaspoon crushed red pepper flakes
⅛ teaspoon cumin
⅛ teaspoon black pepper

Peppered Pistachio Dip

Pistachios are creamy nuts that serve as a great base for dip. This ingredient list may seem somewhat uncommon, but the flavors this recipe brings to the table will not disappoint! The hot peppers and lemon juice breathe life into the pistachios, while the nuts add crunch and texture. Try adding diced tomatoes to this dip for a salsa-like version! It is perfect with crudité or slices of crunchy endive lettuce.

Yields 1 cup dip

¼ cup chopped jalapeño
½ cup roasted red peppers (jarred)
¼ cup unsalted, unshelled pistachios
3 tablespoons chopped fresh basil
¼ cup olive oil
1½ tablespoons lemon juice
Salt, to taste

Combine all ingredients in a blender or food processor and mix until desired consistency is reached. Refrigerate until ready to serve.

Spiced-Up Pumpkin Dip

The spiciness and fresh taste of the chili pepper, lime, and Tabasco really complement the pumpkin flavor in this mouthwatering Spiced-Up Pumpkin Dip! Enjoy this tasty treat with crudités, Spicy Sweet Potato Chips (see recipe in this chapter), or as an eye-watering condiment inside some lettuce wraps with a filling of your choice. This pumpkin dish packs a serious punch that you're guaranteed to love!

Yields 32 ounces

6 cups pumpkin (flesh), seeded and cubed
2 tablespoons caraway seeds
¼ cup lime juice
6 tablespoons lemon juice
¼ cup canola oil
1 tablespoon minced garlic
2 tablespoons Tabasco
½ cup chopped parsley
1 tablespoon minced red chili pepper
Salt and pepper, to taste

1. Bring a large pot of water to a boil, add the pumpkin, and cook until it is easily pierced by a fork but still maintains some resistance, about 6–8 minutes.

2. Toast the caraway seeds in a small sauté pan over medium heat for about 2–3 minutes, shaking frequently to prevent them from burning, until they start to release a little smoke.

3. Drain the pumpkin, allow it to cool to room temperature, and combine it with the caraway seeds and all remaining ingredients. Purée in a food processor or blender. Refrigerate until ready to serve.

Amped-Up Apple Butter

This smooth, spiced-up apple butter is irresistible! It is a perfect snack or addition to any meal. It's delicious when served with the Peppery Pork Roast and Spiced Cider–Soaked Roast of Turkey (see Chapter 4). In this pumped-up Paleo dish, the apple cider breaks down the apple slices, and the invigorating fall-flavored spices give this "butter" a ton of sweet heat. This is a perfect recipe to use up leftover apples after apple picking.

Yields about 1 quart

6 apples (preferably Gala or Cortland), sliced
1 cup apple cider
2 teaspoons cinnamon
½ teaspoon ginger
½ teaspoon nutmeg
½ teaspoon allspice
½ teaspoon ground cloves

1. Cook the apple slices and cider in a sauce pot over medium heat, stirring frequently until it comes to a boil. Lower the heat and simmer for about 30 minutes, stirring periodically.

2. Stir in all the spices, and continue simmering for another 30 minutes (and continue to stir). Cook until the slices of apple have broken down and the mixture is thick, and then remove from heat. Use an immersion blender to mix if desired consistency is not reached by stirring.

3. Transfer to 1 large or 4 individual airtight containers, and store in the fridge.

CHAPTER 7
Desserts and Drinks

No matter the season, there's nothing better than a fiery treat that will thrill your palate and make your toes tingle! The spicy desserts found in this chapter are simply the perfect ending to a long, hard day, or just as a delicious finale to one of the many pleasing entrées in Chapter 4. In addition, the desserts in this chapter—ranging from Mexican-Spiced Coffee Cake to Zesty Choco Fudge to Baked Apple Spice—have an innovative twist, and quite a few out-of-the-box ingredients, which will help you concoct an array of elaborate, spicy, and extraordinary confections! Whether they're spiced with seasonings like nutmeg, ginger, cinnamon, cardamom, and cloves, or made spicy with hot peppers, cayenne, black pepper, and many more fresh herbs, these Paleo sweet treats are breathtakingly phenomenal! In addition, you'll also find a variety of beverages like Raspberry Habanero Margaritas, Spiced Eggnog, and a Virgin Spicy Sangria that will help you wash down these decadent desserts. So sit back, relax, and let your taste buds embark on an amazing adventure!

Pumpkin Spice Custard

This Paleo-approved Pumpkin Spice Custard tastes just like pumpkin pie—without the crust of course, but who needs that? This is a rich and creamy, full-bodied blend of melt-in-your-mouth pleasure. This dessert is packed full of the always-delectable union of cinnamon, ginger, nutmeg, and cardamom. These delicious spices fuse gloriously with the sugary mix of pumpkin, honey, vanilla, and coconut used in this recipe. This dish is sure to surpass all of your expectations and your taste buds will be yearning for more . . . and more . . . and more.

Serves 5

1 cup canned pumpkin purée
1 teaspoon cinnamon
½ teaspoon ground ginger
¼ teaspoon nutmeg
¼ teaspoon cardamom
Pinch sea salt
2 whole eggs
2 egg whites
¼ cup raw organic honey or
   pure maple syrup
1 teaspoon vanilla extract
1 cup coconut or almond milk

1. Preheat the oven to 350°F, and set a pot of water on the stove to boil.

2. Combine the pumpkin and all the spices in a large bowl. In a separate bowl, beat the eggs and egg whites, and add the honey or syrup, vanilla, and milk to the eggs. Pour the egg mixture into the pumpkin mixture and mix well.

3. Pour the formed custard mix into five individual small ramekins, then place all the bowls into a baking pan. Pour the hot water (from step 1) into the pan around the ramekins, which should cover more than half of the height of the ramekins.

4. Bake for 60 minutes, or until a toothpick inserted into the center comes out clean. Enjoy warm or chilled.

Baked Apple Spice

This wonderfully warm, sweet, decadent yet healthy dessert recipe has just the right amount of zing. The rich, smooth, sugary taste of the maple syrup is accented beautifully by the spice blend made up of cinnamon, nutmeg, and cloves. It's a delicious exemplification of the perfect marriage between sweet and spice! Enjoy.

1. Preheat the oven 350°F. Peel the skin of the apples down about 1" from the top. Level the bottoms and arrange in a baking dish.

2. Combine cinnamon, nutmeg, and cloves in a small bowl.

3. Fill the cavity of each apple with 1 table-spoon of the maple syrup, 1 tablespoon of the coconut butter, and a dash of the spice mixture.

4. Fill the baking dish with water and bake, basting often, for 45–50 minutes, or until the apples have reached desired tenderness.

Serves 6

6 large Cortland apples, washed and cored
½ teaspoon ground cinnamon
¼ teaspoon ground nutmeg
¼ teaspoon ground cloves
6 tablespoons maple syrup
6 tablespoons coconut butter, softened and divided
¾ cup water

🔥 DESSERT FOR BREAKFAST!

This astounding apple recipe works well for breakfast too, and is sure to have you jumping out of bed in the morning! Add a serving of coconut or almond yogurt for some protein, and a sprinkling of almond slivers or chopped pecans for an added heart-healthy crunch, and voilà! Now you've got a complete breakfast packed with fiber, vitamin C, omega-3s, calcium, complex carbohydrates, and whole lot of fabulous flavor.

Carrot Spice Cake

If you've never tried a Paleo version of carrot cake, you are in for a real treat! In this recipe, fresh, sweet carrots lend themselves exquisitely to a moist, fluffy, and deliciously spiced cake. The divinely rich and creamy Cinnamon-Ginger-Almond Butter (see Chapter 6) blends marvelously with the additional zest from the fresh nutmeg, cloves, and cinnamon. The walnut and coconut topping give this cake the perfect sweet ending.

Yields 1 (8" × 8") cake

1½ cups blanched almond flour
½ teaspoon sea salt
½ teaspoon baking soda
2 teaspoons cinnamon
½ teaspoon ground nutmeg
½ teaspoon ground cloves
¼ cup unsweetened shredded coconut
3 large eggs
3 tablespoons melted coconut oil
¼ cup Cinnamon-Ginger-Almond Butter (see Chapter 6)
¼ cup raw organic honey
1½ cups grated carrots
½ cup chopped walnuts

1. Preheat the oven to 325°F.

2. In large bowl, combine the almond flour, salt, baking soda, cinnamon, nutmeg, cloves, and shredded coconut with wire whisk. In a separate bowl, mix together the eggs, coconut oil, Cinnamon-Ginger-Almond Butter, and honey, and mix well. Add the carrots and mix on low. Combine the ingredients from both bowls, and mix well.

3. Spread batter into a pre-greased 8" × 8" baking pan and bake for 40–50 minutes. When the cake has cooled, top with walnuts and a dusting of unsweetened shredded coconut, if desired.

Spicy Mexican Chocolate Mousse

An exquisitely divine taste of heaven, this rich and creamy dessert is pure pleasure! The avocado in this recipe creates an irresistibly smooth, velvety feel; it's like nothing you've ever experienced. In addition, the magnificent blend of sugar and spice—the dark chocolate, agave, honey, and vanilla— blend marvelously with the zesty flavors of the cinnamon and chili powder. This spicy dish is unforgettably out of this world!

1. Melt the chocolate chips over a double boiler until smooth and creamy. This entails boiling water in a sauce pot while melting chocolate chips in a pot, on top of the boiling water.

2. Place the avocado flesh, the melted chocolate, agave, honey, coconut milk, cocoa powder, vanilla, cinnamon, and chili powder into a food processor or blender. Blend for 1–2 minutes or until a smooth, chocolatey mixture has formed.

3. Scoop mousse into 4–6 small individual bowls and refrigerate for 1–2 hours to set. Serve garnished with fresh berries and/or almond slivers.

Yields 4–6 servings

¾ cup 60 percent cacao bittersweet chocolate chips (or dark chocolate chips, 70 percent or higher)

4 very ripe avocados, halved, pitted, and peeled

¼ cup agave nectar

¼ cup raw organic honey

⅓ cup full-fat coconut milk

½ cup cocoa powder

1 tablespoon vanilla extract

1 teaspoon cinnamon

¼ teaspoon chili powder

½ cup fresh berries and/or ¼ cup almond slivers, for garnish

Ginger-Spiced Cupcakes with Pumpkin Spice Frosting

Whoever said the Paleo diet prohibits cupcakes? This spicy, Paleo-friendly dessert is an absolute dream! It's perfect for all those holiday parties, cupcake/cookie swaps, or your best friend's birthday—but these cupcakes are so good, you won't want to limit them to special occasions!

Yields 12 cupcakes (or 24 mini cupcakes)

For Frosting:
1 cup canned coconut cream/milk, full fat, refrigerated overnight (about 2 cans)
Heaping ¼ cup canned pumpkin
3 tablespoons maple syrup
1 teaspoon vanilla
½ teaspoon lemon juice
½ teaspoon pink Himalayan salt
¼ teaspoon cinnamon
¼ teaspoon pumpkin pie spice
¼ teaspoon cloves

For Ginger-Spiced Cupcakes:
3 eggs, beaten
⅔ cup raw organic honey
½ cup coconut oil, melted
1 teaspoon vanilla extract
½ teaspoon maple extract
3 cups almond flour
1 teaspoon baking soda
½ teaspoon baking powder
½ teaspoon cardamom
2 teaspoons ground ginger
2 teaspoons cinnamon
¼ teaspoon ground cloves

1. **For Frosting:** In a tall cup or bowl, add all frosting ingredients. Use a hand mixer to combine and whip the ingredients together. Place the frosting in the refrigerator, uncovered, to thicken for at least 30 minutes while preparing cupcakes.

2. **For Ginger-Spiced Cupcakes:** Preheat the oven to 350°F. In a large bowl, combine the eggs, honey, coconut oil, vanilla extract, and maple extract and beat well. In another bowl, combine all of the dry ingredients and mix well. Combine ingredients from both bowls (wet and dry). Scoop the batter into a greased 12-cupcake pan (or 24-mini cupcake pan), or line with cupcake liners, then bake for 20 minutes. Reduce the heat to 225°F, and continue baking for an additional 15–25 minutes. Allow cupcakes to cool completely before removing from pan and frosting.

Spicy Grilled Peaches

This dish is a wonderfully simple grilled dessert (or side dish!), made from sweet, juicy peaches; but it's quite a versatile recipe that could be made just as easily using a variety of fruit. A pinch of chili powder gives these fruity favorites a little spark of fire, and accentuates the sweeter spices brilliantly! These are fabulous when eaten warm and topped with some cold whipped coconut cream.

1. Preheat the grill to high heat. While the grill is preheating, mix all the ingredients together, except for the peaches.

2. Place the peaches in a bowl and pour the sauce mixture over them, evenly coating all of the peaches. Then place the peaches on the heated grill grates carefully, and make sure they don't fall through the grate.

3. Grill the peaches for about 5 minutes per side, on all three sides, or until they are nicely charred. Allow to cool prior to serving and top with some whipped cream!

Serves 4

1 tablespoon coconut oil, melted
2 teaspoons raw organic honey, melted
½ teaspoon cinnamon
⅛ teaspoon nutmeg
⅛ teaspoon chili powder
Primal Whipped Cream (see recipe in this chapter), for garnish (optional)
3 white peaches, pitted and quartered

Primal Whipped Cream

There is nothing better than a scoop of cold, homemade whipped cream! Cinnamon and cardamom team up in this recipe, adding lots of pizzazz to this perfectly spiced, sweet treat. A great addition to any dessert, try this Paleo-friendly whipped cream atop any of the desserts within this chapter; stir in a dollop or two in a cup of Spiced Hot Chai-colate, Masala-Spiced Chai Tea, or the Paleo Pumpkin Spice Latte (see recipes in this chapter); or as a garnish for the delicious smoothies in Chapter 1.

Yields 1½ cups

1 can full-fat coconut milk
1 tablespoon vanilla extract
½ teaspoon cinnamon
2 tablespoons raw organic honey
⅛ teaspoon cardamom

1. Refrigerate can of coconut milk overnight. This will cause the cream to separate from the milk.

2. The next day, open the can of coconut milk (from the bottom), pour out the milk to a separate container (and set aside or discard), and scrape the cream out of the can into a bowl. Add the four remaining ingredients, and whip together with a hand mixer until fluffy. Store in the refrigerator until ready to serve.

♨ NATIONAL WHIPPED CREAM DAY!

This national "food" holiday falls on January 5, the birthday of the founder of Reddi-wip, Aaron "Bunny" Lapin, as a way to celebrate his contribution to the dessert world. However, many consider this "holiday" to be in bad taste, claiming it to be a celebration of lavishness. The notion has deemed many to consider this declared "holiday" to be insensitive, given the severity of hunger worldwide.

Spiced Gingerbread Loaf

This Spiced Gingerbread Loaf is a soft, moist, spiced cake that is so satisfying, it needs nothing more than a scoop of the Compelling Coconut Concoction or a blazing hot mug of Spiced Hot Chai-colate (see recipes in this chapter) to make your night complete. You may only think of serving gingerbread around the holidays, but this treat is much too tasty to only enjoy during the holiday season! Feel free to make it whenever the craving hits—and enjoy.

1. Preheat the oven to 350°F. Combine the almond flour, baking soda, salt, ginger, cinnamon, and pepper in a medium bowl, and stir to blend. In a separate bowl, combine the eggs, ¼ cup coconut oil, and honey together, and then add these to the dry ingredients.

2. Add the remaining 1 teaspoon coconut oil and the chopped pieces of pear to a frying pan and sauté for 4–5 minutes, or until soft.

3. Line a 9" × 5" loaf pan with parchment paper. Add ¼ of the above batter from the bowl, and spread evenly over the bottom of the pan. Add ¼ of the sautéed pears over the batter, and then pour the rest of the batter into the loaf pan. Add the remaining sautéed pears. Bake for 1 hour.

4. Remove from heat and allow to cool for 10 minutes in the pan. Remove by taking hold of the parchment paper and pulling it out of the loaf pan. Cut into slices of desired thickness and enjoy!

Yields 8–10 servings

3 cups blanched almond flour
¾ teaspoon baking soda
½ teaspoon salt
3 teaspoons ground ginger
1 teaspoon cinnamon
⅛ teaspoon black pepper
3 eggs
¼ cup plus 1 teaspoon coconut oil
¼ cup raw organic honey
1 small pear, peeled and chopped into small pieces

Mexican-Spiced Coffee Cake

Who doesn't love a nice, luscious, good ol' piece of chocolate cake? The decadent chocolatey flavor here downright eliminates the need for frosting. Instead, this recipe lets the cake be the star, which is how it should be! This cake's remarkably sweet taste and distinctive aroma is beautifully enhanced by the cinnamon spice and a bit of pep from the cayenne, which turns plain old cake into an astonishingly pleasing, sensational creation!

Yields 10–14 servings

⅓ cup raw cocoa powder

⅓ cup plus 1 tablespoon almond flour

1 teaspoon cinnamon

½ teaspoon cayenne pepper, or to taste

½ teaspoon salt

½ teaspoon baking soda

6 eggs

1 cup raw organic honey

2 teaspoons vanilla

½ cup extra-virgin coconut oil, melted

3 ounces unsweetened baking chocolate (100 percent), melted

1. Preheat the oven to 325°F and line a 9" × 5" loaf pan with greased wax paper.

2. Sift cocoa powder, almond flour, cinnamon, cayenne, salt, and baking soda into a small bowl. In a separate bowl, combine the eggs, honey, and vanilla and blend with a blender or an immersion blender. Add the melted coconut oil and unsweetened baking chocolate and blend for 1 more minute. Add the dry ingredients, and continue mixing.

3. Pour the batter into the prepared loaf pan and bake for 50–60 minutes. Let the cake cool completely before removing from the pan.

Racy Ruby Red Rhubarb

A deliciously tart after-dinner sweet treat that has just the perfect splash of spice makes this Racy Ruby Red Rhubarb oh-so-nice! The allspice and ginger create a little kick while accentuating the delightful hints of sweetness from the honey and fresh fruit. Top this dish off with a dash of cinnamon if you wish, and try some pecans and dried cranberries in place of the almonds—or perhaps a medley of all three!

Combine all ingredients except the almonds and yogurt in a saucepan, bring to a simmer, and turn the heat to low. Cook on low heat for 10–15 minutes until soft. Serve warm with some yogurt and toasted almonds.

Serves 4

2½ cups diced rhubarb
⅔ cup diced pineapple
Juice of 1 orange
½ teaspoon allspice
½ teaspoonginger
2 tablespoons raw organic honey
1–2 ounces water
4 tablespoons toasted slivered almonds
½ cup coconut or almond milk yogurt

🔥 RHUBARB RUMORS

Although rhubarb is technically a vegetable, it frequently assumes the role of fruit in desserts, pies, tarts, sauces, and jams. Rhubarb is easy to grow, but needs cool weather to thrive and extreme cold weather damages the plant. The leaves of rhubarb are poisonous and must be removed. You only eat the stalks, which have a rich tart flavor.

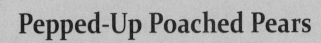

Pepped-Up Poached Pears

What a deliciously spicy, warming dessert! The spices in this delectable dish perfectly accent the pears and sweet honey while pepping up the flavor. You can store these delights for up to 5 days, refrigerated. The longer they sit, the deeper the flavor becomes. These are best enjoyed warm on a cold winter's day. Top with a dollop of pure maple syrup and a sprinkle of toasted shredded coconut.

Serves 4

Juice of 2 large oranges
Zest of 1 orange
3½ cups water
½ cup raw organic honey
3–4 cloves
1 star anise
1 tablespoon cinnamon
1 teaspoon minced ginger
1 teaspoon vanilla extract
4 Bosc pears (somewhat firm)

1. Combine all ingredients (except for the pears) in a medium-large sauce pot. Turn heat to medium-high. Peel the pears evenly, and leave whole with stems. Add each pear to liquid after peeling. Bring to a boil and turn down the heat. Simmer for about 20–25 minutes. To test if pears are done, pierce with a knife. If it slices through easily, remove the pears from the mixture.

2. If not eating right away, place pears in the refrigerator in a sealed container (eat chilled or heat in the microwave when ready to eat if you prefer a warm dessert). They will absorb more flavors the longer they sit. If eating right away, remove from heat and allow spiced orange-honey mixture to simmer until it thickens and is reduced by at least half. Pour it over the pears when serving, and top with your favorite Paleo topper!

♨ PAIRING THE PEARS

These Pepped-Up Poached Pears are great when eaten warmed or chilled, and can be garnished with many Paleo-friendly toppings! Try roasting a handful of almonds and macadamia nuts with cinnamon and add to this pear dessert for crunch. If you want a creamier finish, try a dollop of the following mixture:

- *¼ cup unsweetened coconut yogurt*
- *1 teaspoon raw organic honey*
- *2 drops vanilla extract*
- *Pinch cinnamon*

Gingered Pumpkin Trifles

There is no way to resist these creamy, crunchy, spicy delights! They have a spiced-up pumpkin pie flavor, without any of the guilt of traditional pie. This layered dessert is perfect for the fall, but try different layers for other seasons! Try adding other layers for more texture and different tastes. For variation, try layering bananas, other nuts (like pecans or walnuts), or even dark chocolate shavings. This recipe is best served chilled.

1. In a medium bowl, mix pumpkin purée, honey, cinnamon, cardamom, nutmeg, pumpkin pie spice, and 2 tablespoons coconut yogurt together. (Hint: Try whipping with an immersion blender to make it fluffier.)

2. In a separate small mixing bowl, combine remaining yogurt and maple syrup until blended.

3. Start building your trifles! In small dessert glasses, place a spoonful of the pumpkin mixture on the bottom. On top of the pumpkin mixture, put a spoonful of the coconut yogurt mixture. Top with the chopped almonds and toasted coconut. Repeat this process until your glass is full and you have a layered dessert!

Serves 2

1 (28-ounce) can pumpkin purée
1 tablespoon raw organic honey
1 teaspoon cinnamon
1 teaspoon ground cardamom
½ teaspoon ground nutmeg
½ teaspoon pumpkin pie spice
1 cup unsweetened coconut yogurt, divided use
1 tablespoon pure maple syrup
1 cup almonds, chopped
1 cup shredded coconut (lightly toasted for crunch)

Cardamom Carrot Custard

This delicious, Indian-inspired dessert is highly pleasing to the taste buds! The sweet carrots are the main ingredient in this dish and really blend well with the added spice from the cardamom. Try adding additional savory spices to this recipe, like thyme or sage, and use as a dinner side dish. Carrots are wonderfully nutritious vegetables, so incorporating them into a dessert makes for a healthy after-dinner treat!

Serves 4

2 tablespoons clarified butter
8 large carrots, peeled and chopped
1 cup unsweetened coconut milk
½ cup pure maple syrup
1 teaspoon ground cardamom
1 teaspoon vanilla extract
Pinch ground ginger
½ cup chopped pecans

1. In a large stainless steel sauté pan, melt the clarified butter over medium heat. Add the carrots when the butter has turned to liquid, and turn the heat up a bit to get the carrots sizzling. Cook for 5–7 minutes, then turn the heat down and simmer.

2. While the carrots are sautéing, slowly heat the coconut milk over low heat in a small saucepan. Add all remaining ingredients to the milk (except the chopped nuts and the carrots) and whisk until well blended. Once this milk mixture is heated through, add it to the carrots. Simmer for 30 minutes, so carrots soften and the flavors have a chance to meld, then turn off the heat to cool slightly.

3. Blend the ingredients with an immersion blender once it has slightly cooled until the mixture is a chunky purée. Serve warmed, topped with the chopped pecans.

♦ TRADITIONAL HALVA

Halva is a traditional Indian/Middle Eastern dessert made up of many different types of ingredients. The most frequently prepared version is made up of carrots, milk, sugar, ghee (clarified butter), and cardamom; however, there are many countries that make it with semolina, sunflower seeds, chickpeas, and other types of vegetables like squash. There are many ways of preparing this delectable dish, but without fail, it always ends up a sweet and savory treat!

Blazin' Bananas

These Blazin' Bananas are a warm, sweet treat with a huge punch of spice from the cayenne pepper! It leaves a small amount of heat on your tongue, which is quickly extinguished with your next bite of banana. This dish is a great snack, dessert, or side to an entrée. This dish tastefully accents both ham and turkey when served as a side dish, or you can try adding chopped almonds and cashews for extra sustenance from the healthy fats when serving this as a dessert.

1. Mix all the spices together in a bowl. Preheat your grill to high heat, and allow the grates to get hot.

2. With a marinade brush, coat the bananas with the melted clarified butter, and then place onto the grill grates, flat (cut) side down. Sprinkle the top with the spice mixture, and grill for about 1–2 minutes before flipping. Grill on the other side for another 1–2 minutes, until both sides are charred and the banana is slightly softened. Serve with a sprinkle of cinnamon.

Serves 4

1 teaspoon cinnamon, plus more for garnish
½ teaspoon nutmeg
Pinch cayenne pepper
4 large bananas, peeled and halved lengthwise
2 tablespoons clarified butter, melted

🔥 FLAMBÉING FOR FLAVOR!

This is a great recipe to be creative with and try something you most likely don't do every day. To give this dessert some added flavor (and spirit!), place a large sauté pan over high heat. Once the pan is heated, add the grilled bananas and about ¼ cup of spiced rum to the pan. Heat for about 30 seconds and tilt the pan slightly so the rum catches fire. If using an electric stove, light a match near the mixture. Let flame for just a moment and serve!

Spiced Oranges

A tangy twist on the vitamin C–packed fruit, these Spiced Oranges will soon become a favorite! Traditionally known for their sweet, juicy flavor, oranges actually have quite a bit of versatility. Cinnamon, cloves, and honey give these succulent snacks a unique flavorful kick! Get your daily serving of immune-enhancing vitamin C with these spiced sweet treats.

Yields 2 Servings

¼ cup 100 percent grape juice
3 tablespoons water
1 tablespoon raw organic honey
1 lemon slice
1 small (about 1") cinnamon stick
1 whole clove
2 medium oranges, peeled and sectioned
Fresh mint, to taste

1. Combine the grape juice, water, honey, lemon, cinnamon stick, and clove in a saucepan and cook over medium heat until it starts to thicken slightly, about 15 minutes. Add the oranges and simmer for 1 minute, then pour into a bowl and refrigerate.

2. Discard the lemon, cinnamon stick, and the clove before serving, and garnish with fresh mint.

Zesty Choco Fudge

This dense dessert is a chocolatey, nutty delight! It is an ultra-moist, sweet and spiced recipe that is easy to make and stores well for a snack. Try different nuts in this recipe, such as almonds or pecans, or even sunflower seeds! For a spicier version, add a pinch of chipotle powder, which is a spice commonly added to cocoa powder.

1. Combine all ingredients in a blender and pulse until a crumbly texture is reached. This mixture should be easy to manipulate and shape when touched.

2. Line an 8" × 8" glass dish with parchment paper. Add the mixture to the dish, and press and flatten into an even square. Place it in the refrigerator to harden, and slice it into small cubes when ready to serve.

Yields approximately 18–20 bite-size pieces

1½ cups walnuts
1 cup dates, pitted
½ cup almond butter
3 tablespoons honey
1 teaspoon vanilla extract
¼ cup cocoa powder
½ teaspoon allspice
½ teaspoon ground ginger

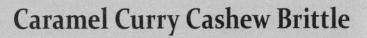

Caramel Curry Cashew Brittle

This recipe utilizes a Paleo-friendly, sugar-free caramel sauce that pairs perfectly with curry and vanilla bean. It is a sweet and crunchy treat with a Middle-Eastern twist! This is an easy, candy-like recipe that will be sure to satisfy any sweet tooth. Use it as a crunchy topping for the Compelling Coconut Concoction ice cream (see recipe in this chapter).

Yields about 2–2½ cups brittle

1½ cups raw organic honey
½ cup pure maple syrup
½ teaspoon baking soda
¼ cup clarified butter
½ teaspoon vanilla bean paste
1 teaspoon curry powder
2 cups chopped cashews
   (roasted for richer flavor)
Pinch sea salt

1. In a medium sauce pot, heat the honey and maple syrup over medium-low heat until it reaches approximately 275°F with a candy thermometer. Next, stir in the baking soda, butter, vanilla bean paste, and curry powder. Whisk ingredients until the butter is melted, and then turn the heat off (but keep the sauce pot over the warm stovetop). This mixture may bubble while heated, so be cautious to remove from heat, stir, and place back on the heat to prevent from bubbling over.

2. Place the chopped cashews in a parchment paper–lined 9" × 9" pan. Pour the caramel-like mixture evenly over the nuts, top with sea salt, and place in the freezer to chill for a minimum of 30 minutes. Break it into chunks and preserve in the freezer until ready to serve, as the brittle becomes sticky if left at room temperature.

🔥 BE BRAVE WITH BRITTLE!

Curry and cashews are an amazing combination of spice and crunch in this recipe, but if you are looking to change it up a bit, try other spices and nuts instead! Use almond slivers and cinnamon for a wintery treat, or pecans and pumpkin pie spice in the fall. To be super creative, pour this honeyed mixture over 2 cups of the Indian Savory Spice Nuts (see Chapter 2).

Cinnamon-Spiced Coconut Bark

A wonderful, rich, creamy, and spiced sweet treat with a little bit of crunch, this Cinnamon-Spiced Coconut Bark is substantial enough to keep you sated, yet so sensational that you'll immediately want more! This dish is an amazing collaboration of coconut, almonds, and walnuts; sweetness from cacao; and just the right amount of zest from the ginger, cinnamon, carob powder, and cardamom.

1. Line a small baking dish or loaf pan with plastic wrap. Place all ingredients except the cacao nibs in a food processor or blender, and process until smooth and almost liquid, which will take up to 10 minutes.

2. Transfer the mixture to a medium bowl and allow to cool to room temperature (as the food processing warms it up a bit), about 15–20 minutes. Once it's cooled, stir in the cacao nibs.

3. Transfer the mixture to the baking dish and smooth the top, then refrigerate or freeze until firm.

4. Remove the bark by flipping the pan upside down, and removing the plastic and the cold, firm coconut bark. Remove plastic and cut into chunks. Store in the refrigerator in an airtight container for up to 1 month.

Yields 12 servings

2 cups unsweetened, dried shredded coconut
½ cup walnut halves, lightly toasted
½ cup natural almonds, lightly toasted
25 drops liquid stevia
1½ teaspoons cinnamon
1 tablespoon carob powder
¼ teaspoon cardamom
¾ teaspoon ground ginger
⅓ cup cacao nibs, chopped

Coconut Sweet Potato Bites— With a Bite!

With a luscious blend of dried fruit, heart-healthy nuts, super-nutritious sweet potatoes, and a pinch of pep, courtesy of cinnamon, cloves, and cardamom, these zesty, super-satisfying truffles are spectacular! Enjoy as an easy post-meal snack, or as recovery fuel following a morning workout. Just be cautious; these are so good it's hard to eat just one!

Yields 8–12 round bites

- 1 cup pitted dates
- 1 cup raw hazelnuts
- 2 small sweet potatoes, fully cooked, skin removed
- 1 tablespoon coconut oil
- ½ teaspoon cinnamon
- ¼ teaspoon ground cloves
- ¼ teaspoon cardamom
- 1–2 tablespoons chopped cranberries
- 1 tablespoon sesame seeds
- 1 tablespoon raw cacao powder

1. Place the dates, hazelnuts, sweet potatoes, coconut oil, cinnamon, cloves, and cardamom in a food processor or blender, and mix until evenly combined and smooth.

2. Combine the chopped cranberries, sesame seeds, and cacao powder in a small bowl and mix gently. Roll the dough into round bites of desired size, and roll each one in the dried cranberries, sesame seeds, and cacao powder. Store in an airtight container in the refrigerator for up to 2 weeks.

Compelling Coconut Concoction

This sweet, cool, refreshing treat is perfect on a hot summer's day, and it's an easy, fresh way of using coconut milk to create a delicious Paleo ice cream! The allspice, cardamom, and vanilla bean paste add a peppery sweetness to every spoonful, and you should let your creativity run wild and add some fruit or additional spice. This concoction has endless possibilities. It's best with chopped, baked apples and cinnamon, or honey and bananas. Try topping it with a sprinkling of crushed nuts or toasted coconut flakes.

1. In a large bowl, mix the eggs with a hand-held mixer for about 1 minute on low, until the eggs are frothy and well blended. Add in the maple syrup, vanilla bean paste, and spices and mix on low for another minute, until well blended. Finally, add in the coconut milk and mix on low for 1–2 minutes. (If you do not have a handheld mixer, you can vigorously whisk the ingredients together.)

2. If you have an ice cream maker, pour mixed ingredients in and use as instructed to make ice cream. If you do not have an ice cream maker, pour your ingredients into a metal pan and place it in the freezer. About every 45 minutes, remove from freezer and stir the ingredients. The mixture will continue to become increasingly frozen. Repeat this step until you reach a desired, creamy consistency.

Yields approximately 3 cups

2 eggs
½ cup pure maple syrup
1 tablespoon vanilla bean paste
½ teaspoon ground cardamom
Pinch allspice
2 (14-ounce) cans coconut milk

🔥 VANILLA BEAN PASTE

Vanilla bean paste is a delicious ingredient in many desserts. It is a spiced-up version of vanilla extract, as it contains ground vanilla beans. It is much thicker than vanilla extract, but can be used in the same measurement. For example, 1 teaspoon of vanilla extract is equivalent to 1 teaspoon of vanilla bean paste. The addition of this ingredient to the coconut ice cream adds little black specks of punch and adds incredible flavor.

Minty Melon Sorbet

This Minty Melon Sorbet is a cool, satisfying treat on a hot day! It is best enjoyed in the summer when melon is in season and extra juicy. The mint and thyme add a zesty, herbal flavor to the sweet melon, and taste delicious when this frosty dessert hits your lips. This recipe is versatile; try blending it with ice for a sorbet-inspired smoothie variation.

Serves 3–4

2 cups melon (watermelon, honeydew, or cantaloupe)
Juice of 2 oranges
3 tablespoons water
2 tablespoons raw organic honey
4–5 sprigs fresh mint, chopped (plus extra, for garnish, if desired)
½ teaspoon fresh thyme, chopped
Pinch lime zest

1. Blend the melon in a food processor until it reaches a somewhat smooth consistency. In a medium sauce pot, combine all other ingredients over medium heat. Stir frequently, and let mixture simmer for about 10 minutes. Remove the pot from the heat and let it cool. Add the orange mixture to the puréed melon in the food processor and blend until smooth.

2. Place all the ingredients into an ice cream maker. If you do not have access to an ice cream maker, pour the mixture onto a clean metal baking sheet and freeze until it sets. Add it to a food processor again once frozen, with a splash of water to help purée it to a smooth mixture. Enjoy with fresh sprigs of mint as a garnish.

🔥 SORBET SAMPLES

This sorbet recipe is not limited to melons and mint! Instead, try a medley of fruits and herbs to create your own tasty dessert. Replace the melon and mint/thyme with equal parts mixed berries and chopped jalapeño/cilantro. Or try a citrus version, with peaches and mangos and a hint of cinnamon and ginger!

Spiced Hot Chai-colate

This spiced-up version of Paleo hot chocolate is absolutely fabulous! Chai tea is used in this recipe to bring the spice, but you can substitute in any tea of your choice. If you want to try an alternative to the chai tea, add a medley of spices to your preference. Spices like cloves, cinnamon, ginger, and a hint of black pepper will blend wonderfully!

1. Add the tea to ⅛ cup of hot water and let it steep.

2. To a small saucepan, add the remaining ⅛ cup of hot water and the cacao powder, and whisk to combine. Stir in the milk and heat until warm. Add the coconut oil and then add the honey, to taste.

3. Remove the tea bag from the water, add the steeped tea to the pan, and continue heating until the coconut oil has dissolved and steam is rising from the pan. Transfer to a large mug, and top off with a dollop of whipped coconut cream and dash of cinnamon, if desired!

Yields 1 (9-ounce) cup

1 bag chai tea
¼ cup hot water, divided use
1–2 tablespoons cacao powder
1 cup almond or coconut milk
1 tablespoon coconut oil
Raw organic honey, to taste
1–2 tablespoons whipped
  coconut cream, optional
¼ teaspoon cinnamon, optional

Masala-Spiced Chai Tea

The aroma of this homemade tea will fill your home with warmth and love. Warm up with a steaming mug of this spiced-up chai on a cold wintery day—or whenever you crave a sweet, peppery beverage. The simmering spice from the blend of ginger, cloves, star anise, and ginger packs a whole lot of flavor into just one sip!

Serves 3

1 whole cinnamon stick
6 cardamom pods (crushed for stronger taste)
4 whole cloves
4 whole black peppercorns
5–6 thin slices fresh ginger
1 piece star anise
3½ cups water
2 tea bags (black tea)
2 tablespoons raw organic honey
1½ cups coconut milk

1. In a medium saucepan, combine cinnamon, cardamom, cloves, peppercorns, ginger, star anise, and water. Bring to a boil.

2. Turn down heat and simmer for 5–7 minutes until fragrant, then remove from heat, turn off burners, and let cool/steep for 10 minutes.

3. Add tea bags, return to stove on medium-high heat, bring to a boil, and then remove from heat completely, and let steep another 2–3 minutes.

4. Add honey and coconut milk and serve into mugs through a fine mesh sieve.

🌶 CARDAMOM

Cardamom is sold in a ground form, as seeds, or in the form of whole pods (which contain the seeds). The richest cardamom flavor comes from taking the seed from the shell and grinding it fresh. Use a mortar and pestle to grind the little black cardamom seeds, and sit back and smell the sweet aroma!

Paleo Pumpkin Spice Latte

A seasonal favorite, this Paleo Pumpkin Spice Latte recipe is so simple, you'll want to make it every morning! This recipe uses real pumpkin, which gives a much more prominent flavor compared to the artificial ingredients used at the mainstream coffee chains. The vanilla and honey bring sweetness, and the cinnamon and nutmeg bring the spice—and the amounts of each can be adjusted to precisely meet your individual taste. Allspice can be used in place of the nutmeg here, and decaf espresso, coffee, or decaf coffee can be substituted for espresso. Enjoy at home in your own kitchen, and skip the drive-through altogether!

1. In a saucepan, heat the coconut (or almond) milk, pumpkin, and honey until it is bubbling and steaming. Remove from heat, and stir in vanilla, cinnamon, and nutmeg.

2. Divide between two coffee cups (or one really large one), then pour in the espresso. Add a dollop of whipped coconut cream and a pinch of cocoa powder (and more cinnamon, to taste).

Yields 1–2 lattes

1 cup coconut or almond milk
1½ tablespoons puréed pumpkin
2–3 tablespoons raw organic honey
1 tablespoon vanilla extract
¼ teaspoon cinnamon, plus more to taste, for garnish
Pinch nutmeg
½ cup brewed espresso
2 tablespoons whipped coconut cream
Pinch cocoa powder

Blistering Bloody Mary Mix

This Blistering Bloody Mary Mix is a hot and spicy morning concoction, perfect on the rocks, alone, or with alcohol added. The savory flavor offered from the Dijon mustard, Tabasco sauce, and fresh basil will leave you thirsty for more. This works great as a breakfast juice during the week or as an adult beverage alongside brunch on the weekends!

Serves 4 (yields 1 pitcher with ice)

1 can ground peeled tomatoes
1½ cups vegetable juice
¼ cup Dijon mustard
¼ cup lime juice
2 tablespoons horseradish
2 tablespoons Tabasco sauce
1 teaspoon celery seed
½ teaspoon red pepper flakes
½ teaspoon sea salt and black pepper
Limes, jalapeños, and celery, for garnish
4 ounces vodka or gin (optional)

1. Combine all ingredients in an extra-large glass measuring cup or pitcher. Stir ingredients with a wooden spoon, then use an immersion blender to blend ingredients until smooth and frothy.

2. Serve in a glass with ice by itself or with an ounce of vodka or gin. Garnish with a lime, a pickled jalapeño, and celery.

🔥 IN GOOD SPIRITS

Traditionally, vodka is the most common choice of liquor for the alcoholic version of a Bloody Mary, and these versions of this drink have also been referred to as Red Hammers. Historically, however, gin is the liquor of choice. Garnishes also vary and often include veggies like olives, celery, green beans, pickled okra, cucumber slices, pepperoni sticks, dill pickles, and more. Choose wisely!

Spiced Eggnog

The holiday season is simply not the same without a creamy, nutmeg-spiced glass of eggnog. This Paleo version is just as tasty and creamy as traditional eggnog. The nutmeg and allspice nicely accent the feisty vanilla bean flavor. Add a shot of your favorite holiday spirit (spiced rum is a favorite of ours), and turn this liquid refresher into a warming Christmas cocktail!

1. In a large mixing bowl, mix the egg yolks with a handheld mixer on medium speed (or whisk vigorously), until they lighten in color and become frothy. Slowly add in maple syrup, vanilla bean paste, and the spices (not including the cinnamon sticks) and whisk until well blended. Add in coconut milk and almond milk and stir.

2. Pour the mixture into a medium-large saucepan over low heat. Add in the cinnamon sticks and stir frequently. Heat the mixture extremely slowly, as the eggs will scramble if heated too quickly. Simmer until the mixture thickens and coats the back of a spoon when dipped.

3. Remove the cinnamon sticks and place mixture in a sealed container in the refrigerator to chill. Serve cold with a pinch of cinnamon on top.

Serves 4

5 egg yolks
2 tablespoons pure maple syrup
1½ tablespoons vanilla bean paste
1 teaspoon ground cinnamon plus more for garnish
1 teaspoon fresh ground nutmeg
¼ teaspoon allspice
2 cups canned coconut milk
2 cups almond milk
2 whole cinnamon sticks
Cinnamon, to taste

Spiced Christmas Cocktail

This zippy version of the traditional Hot Toddy is a light, spicy, citrus cocktail; perfect on a cold winter's day or when shared over dessert with family and friends at a holiday party. The apple cider and honey softly sweeten the tea, and the cinnamon and star anise bring the spice. The whiskey in this recipe is optional, as this "cocktail" can be enjoyed alcohol-free any time of day.

Serves 3–4

4 cups water

4 tea bags (green or herbal tea works well)

3–4 ounces whiskey (optional)

½ cup pure apple cider

¼ cup raw organic honey

3 cinnamon sticks

2 star anise

Juice of 1 lemon

Zest of ½ lemon (save the leftover lemon rind, and set aside for garnish)

1. Bring the water to a boil in a medium-large sauce pot. Once it reaches a rolling boil, add the tea bags and turn heat to low. Let the tea bags steep for about 5 minutes, depending on your preferred strength of tea. Remove and discard tea bags.

2. Add in all the other ingredients and whisk until well blended. You should have a pale, cloudy mixture. Let flavors meld together for an additional 5 minutes. Remove the star anise and cinnamon sticks. Serve hot, garnished with the leftover lemon rind.

Raspberry Habanero Margaritas

Summer will not be the same once you discover these fiery, fruity margaritas! The muddled fruit and pepper create a hot and tart addition to the traditional Mexican cocktail, and the salted rim and fresh lime juice complete this heavenly mixture—providing an irresistible yet guilt-free summer drink. To tame down the spice, try using jalapeños in place of the habanero pepper!

1. Coat the rim of a margarita glass with lime juice, let it dry for a brief moment, and then dip the rim of the glass onto a plate coated with sea salt. Set aside.

2. Place half of the lime juice, lime zest, and raspberries into a large mixer. Using a garlic press, squeeze the chunk of habanero pepper (flesh side down) into the mixer. Use a muddler to grind all of these ingredients together to create a thick, mushy mixture.

3. Add tequila, honey, and ice to the mixer, and shake vigorously for 1–2 minutes to create a frothy pink drink. Pour the liquid into the salt-rimmed margarita glass and top it off with a splash of soda water. Garnish with a fresh lime slice and leftover raspberries!

Serves 1

Juice of 1 lime, divided use

Sea salt, as needed

Pinch lime zest

Handful fresh raspberries, plus more for garnish

1 small slice habanero pepper (The size can vary, depending on desired spice. Start with a slice about the size of a penny.)

2 ounces tequila (use your favorite!)

2 tablespoons raw organic honey

Ice, to taste

Splash soda water (lime-flavored works well)

1 slice lime, for garnish

Sexy Summer Sangria

This cool, summery sangria is smooth and lightly spiced. The honey and ginger give this fruity concoction a deep, sultry layer of flavor that you'll absolutely love. Enjoy on ice as-is, or topped with a splash of soda water to make a spritzer. This drink pairs perfectly with a delicious grilled steak dinner and a colorful summer salad, like the Zesty Mandarin Salad found in Chapter 2.

Serves 4–5

Juice of 2 oranges
3 tablespoons raw organic honey
¼ cup water
1 tablespoon freshly ground ginger
½ teaspoon cinnamon
1 bottle red wine (pinot noir works well)
2 oranges cut into thin slices (remove skin from oranges to eliminate bitterness)
1 peach, pitted and cut into thin slices
1 pear, peeled and cut into thin slices

1. Combine fresh orange juice, honey, water, ginger, and cinnamon in a small sauce pot. Heat over medium heat; whisk to combine all ingredients, and allow the honey to melt. This should only last about 5 minutes. Remove from heat and set aside to cool.

2. Add wine, sliced fruit, and the orange juice mixture to a large pitcher and stir. Refrigerate overnight and serve chilled on ice.

Virgin Spicy Sangria

An incredibly simple sensation, this nonalcoholic white sangria is a tasty thirst quencher. Although it's a cool beverage, the spicy jalapeños really turn up the heat, making this drink just as refreshing in the winter as it is in the summer! There are so many ways you can prepare this tasty treat, so get creative. Use cranberry juice for a red version; or put the kids to bed and bring out the spirits such as a red burgundy wine or spiced rum to spice it up even more!

Add all the ingredients to a large pitcher and stir well to evenly combine. Place the pitcher in the refrigerator to infuse the flavors, and chill for at least 1 hour before serving. Serve chilled and over ice, if desired.

Serves 6–8

6 cups white grape juice
¼ cup freshly squeezed lemon juice
1 cup raspberries
1 medium orange (with skin), sliced
1 medium lemon (with skin), sliced
1 medium lime (with skin), sliced
1 medium apple (with skin), cored, sliced, and halved
1 medium green jalapeño, seeds removed and sliced
Ice, optional

Metric Conversion Chart

VOLUME CONVERSIONS	
U.S. Volume Measure	**Metric Equivalent**
⅛ teaspoon	0.5 milliliter
¼ teaspoon	1 milliliter
½ teaspoon	2 milliliters
1 teaspoon	5 milliliters
½ tablespoon	7 milliliters
1 tablespoon (3 teaspoons)	15 milliliters
2 tablespoons (1 fluid ounce)	30 milliliters
¼ cup (4 tablespoons)	60 milliliters
⅓ cup	90 milliliters
½ cup (4 fluid ounces)	125 milliliters
⅔ cup	160 milliliters
¾ cup (6 fluid ounces)	180 milliliters
1 cup (16 tablespoons)	250 milliliters
1 pint (2 cups)	500 milliliters
1 quart (4 cups)	1 liter (about)
WEIGHT CONVERSIONS	
U.S. Weight Measure	**Metric Equivalent**
½ ounce	15 grams
1 ounce	30 grams
2 ounces	60 grams
3 ounces	85 grams
¼ pound (4 ounces)	115 grams
½ pound (8 ounces)	225 grams
¾ pound (12 ounces)	340 grams
1 pound (16 ounces)	454 grams

OVEN TEMPERATURE CONVERSIONS

Degrees Fahrenheit	Degrees Celsius
200 degrees F	95 degrees C
250 degrees F	120 degrees C
275 degrees F	135 degrees C
300 degrees F	150 degrees C
325 degrees F	160 degrees C
350 degrees F	180 degrees C
375 degrees F	190 degrees C
400 degrees F	205 degrees C
425 degrees F	220 degrees C
450 degrees F	230 degrees C

BAKING PAN SIZES

U.S.	Metric
8 × 1½ inch round baking pan	20 × 4 cm cake tin
9 × 1½ inch round baking pan	23 × 3.5 cm cake tin
11 × 7 × 1½ inch baking pan	28 × 18 × 4 cm baking tin
13 × 9 × 2 inch baking pan	30 × 20 × 5 cm baking tin
2 quart rectangular baking dish	30 × 20 × 3 cm baking tin
15 × 10 × 2 inch baking pan	30 × 25 × 2 cm baking tin (Swiss roll tin)
9 inch pie plate	22 × 4 or 23 × 4 cm pie plate
7 or 8 inch springform pan	18 or 20 cm springform or loose bottom cake tin
9 × 5 × 3 inch loaf pan	23 × 13 × 7 cm or 2 lb narrow loaf or pâté tin
1½ quart casserole	1.5 liter casserole
2 quart casserole	2 liter casserole

INDEX

About the Authors

Emily Dionne, MS, RD, LDN, CSSD, ACSM-HFS, is a registered dietitian and Health and Fitness Specialist, with years of experience in the fields of nutritional science, health and wellness, fitness and sports nutrition, and disease prevention. She is also the author of *The Everything® Paleolithic Diet Slow Cooker Cookbook*. As a registered dietitian, Emily provides medical nutrition therapy and health and nutrition education to hundreds of clients managing or trying to prevent a variety of medical conditions including obesity, diabetes, and heart disease. Her wholehearted commitment to a healthful, yet tastefully enjoyable lifestyle, is a practice she strives to instill among all those she encounters, each and every day. Emily's efforts help guide others along the path toward achieving their fitness goals, and maximizing their nutritional health.

Technical Analyst Erin Ray's life is full of flavor and fun. She spends her evenings in the kitchen experimenting with homegrown vegetables and herbs, aspiring to master culinary greatness through clean eating. She was diagnosed with PCOS about ten years ago, and suffered many of its negative side effects. In 2012, Erin began adhering to the Paleolithic lifestyle, and immediately experienced an improvement in her health. Erin's passion for fresh food and affinity for entertaining friends and family has sparked a lifestyle of health, love, and longevity. Erin resides in Bridgewater, Massachusetts, with her husband C.J.